THE MUSICAL

Book by
LUTHER DAVIS

Songs by
ROBERT WRIGHT and **GEORGE FORREST**

Based on VICKI BAUM'S "GRAND HOTEL"
by arrangement with TURNER ENTERTAINMENT CO.,
owner of the motion picture "GRAND HOTEL"
Additional Music and Lyrics by
MAURY YESTON

Music and Lyric Copyrights

We dedicate the acting edition of
Grand Hotel – The Musical
to
TOMMY TUNE

with immense gratitude for his skill, devotion, genius—
and unfailing personal charm. We owe him five
wonderful productions of our show (so far): Broadway,
International Touring Company, Berlin, London, Japan.

and to the late

MARY LEA JOHNSON

who, with Martin Richards and Sam Crothers, took a
long chance that our show might be as good, or nearly as
good, as we said it was.

and to two other brave gamblers:

our agent and friend

ROBERT LANTZ

and our lawyer and friend

LAWRENCE J. GREENE, ESQ.

IMPORTANT CREDIT AND BILLING REQUIREMENTS

1. (a) All licensees, lessees and producers who have been authorized to present a production of the Play, GRAND HOTEL – The Musical, must give credit to Luther Davis, Robert Wright and George Forrest (as Authors), to Vicki Baum (as author of the basic work), and to Maury Yeston (as contributor of additional music and lyrics) in all programs, advertising and publicity related to the Play.

(b) None of the names of the said individuals shall be on the same line as any other credits.

(c) The credits to be given to each of the above-named individuals shall be arranged and shall read as they appear on the following page. (See 3(b) below.)

2. The names of Luther Davis, Robert Wright and George Forrest shall each appear in the same size type and in equal prominence, and no name other than the title of the Play shall appear in greater size or prominence. The size of the names of Messrs. Davis, Wright and Forrest shall each be no less than 50% of the size of the title of the Play.

3. (a) The names of Vicki Baum and of Maury Yeston shall be in size type smaller than the size type of Luther Davis, Robert Wright and George Forrest, and shall be placed as follows:

The credits to Vicki Baum shall appear below those of Luther Davis, Robert Wright and George Forrest.

The credits to Maury Yeston shall appear below those of Luther Davis, Robert Wright and George Forrest, and of Vicki Baum.

(b) The relative sizes of type used in printing the names of each of the above-named five individuals will be in the same sizes relative to each other as such respective sizes appear in the credits set out on the following page.

Grand HOTEL
THE MUSICAL

Book by
LUTHER DAVIS

Songs by
ROBERT WRIGHT and GEORGE FORREST

Based on VICKI BAUM'S "GRAND HOTEL"

Additional Music and Lyrics by
MAURY YESTON

Grand Hotel — The Musical, book by Luther Davis; songs by Robert Wright and George Forrest; based on Vicki Baum's novel, additional music and lyrics by Maury Yeston, had its premiere performance at the Martin Beck Theatre on November 12, 1989. It was presented by Martin Richards, Mary Lea Johnson, Sam Crothers, Sander Jacobs, Kenneth D. Greenblatt, Paramount Pictures, Jujamcyn Theaters in association with Patty Grubman and Marvin A. Krauss. It was directed and choreographed by Tommy Tune. Associate Producers were Sandra Greenblatt, Martin R. Kaufman and Kim Poster; Production Associate, Kathleen Raitt; General Manager, Joey Parnes; General Press Representative, Judy Jacksina; Musical Coordinator, John Monaco; Casting, Julie Hughes and Barry Moss; Hair Design, Werner Sherer; Orchestrations, Peter Matz; Musical and Vocal Direction, Jack Lee; Music Supervision and Additional Music, Wally Harper; Associate Director, Bruce Lumpkin; Setting Design, Tony Walton; Costume Design, Santo Loquasto; Lighting Design, Jules Fisher; Sound Design, Otts Munderloh. The cast (in order of appearance) was:

Colonel Doctor Ottemschlag	John Wylie
The Doorman	Charles Mandracchia
The Countess & The Gigolo	Yvonne Marceau & Pierre Dulaine
Madame Peepee	Kathi Moss
Rohna, the Grand Concierge	Rex D. Hays
The Bellboys:	
George Strunk	Ken Jennings
Kurt Kronenberg	Keith Crowningshield
Hanns Bittner	Gerrit de Beer
Willibald, Captain	J.J. Epson
Erik, Front Desk	Bob Stillman
The Telephone Operators:	
Hildegarde Bratts	Jennifer Lee Andrews
Sigfriede Holzhiem	Suzanne Henderson
Wolffe Bratts	Lynnette Perry
The Chauffeur	Ben George
Zinnowitz, the Lawyer	Hal Robinson
General Director Preysing, Saxonia Mills	Timothy Jerome
Flaemmchen, the Typist	Jane Krakowski
Otto Kringelein, the Bookkeeper	Michael Jeter
Raffaela, the Confidante	Karen Akers
Sandor, the Impresario	Mitchell Jason
Witt, the Company Manager	Michel Moinot
Elizaveta Grushinskaya, the Ballerina	Liliane Montevecchi
Felix Von Gaigern, the Baron	David Carroll
The Jimmys	David Jackson & Danny Strayhorn
The Scullery Workers:	
Ernest Schmidt	Henry Grossman
Franz Kohl	William Ryall
Werner Holst	David Elledge
Gunther Gustafsson	Walter Willison
The Hotel Courtesan	Suzanne Henderson
Trudie, the Maid	Jennifer Lee Andrews

CASTING BREAKDOWN (PRINCIPALS)

COLONEL-DOCTOR OTTERNSCHLAG (THE DOCTOR) – grievously wounded by gas and shrapnel in WWI; a cynical, ruined man.

FLAEMMCHEN (Neé FRIEDA FLAMM) – a pretty girl who seems to be younger than twenty and has theatrical ambitions.

BARON FELIX VON GAIGERN – young, athletic, charming, optimistic, broke.

OTTO KRINGELEIN – not old, but mortally ill; a bookkeeper from a small town.

CHAUFFEUR - a tough cockney (or Spanish or Italian or Algerian) gangster posing as a chauffeur.

RAFFAELA – confidante, secretary, and sometimes dresser to:

ELIZAVETA GRUSHINSKAYA – the still-beautiful, world-famous, about-to-retire Prima Ballerina.

ERIK – intelligent young assistant concierge, ambitious, about to start a family.

ZINNOWITZ – an attorney in Berlin.

HERMANN PREYSING – General Director of a large textile mill; a solid burgher.

SANDOR – Hungarian theater impresario.

ROHNA – hotel general manager; a martinet.

WITT – company manager of Grushinskaya's ballet troupe.

CHARACTERS
(In Order of Appearance)

The Doorman
Colonel-Doctor Otternschlag
The Countess & The Gigolo (Ballroom Dancers)
Rohna, the Hotel Manager
Erik, Front Desk
The Bellboys:
    Georg Strunk
    Kurt Kronenberg
    Hans Bittner
    Willibald, Captain
The Telephone Operators:
    Hildegarde Bratts
    Sigfriede Holzhiem
    Wolffe Bratts
The Two Jimmys (Black American Entertainers)
The Chauffeur
Zinnowitz, Lawyer
Sandor, Impresario
Witt, Company Manager of Ballet Company
Madame Peepee (Lavatory Attendant)
General Director Preysing, Saxonia Mills
"Flaemmchen," Typist, theatrically ambitious
Otto Kringelein, Bookkeeper
Felix von Gaigern, Baron
Raffaela, Confidante of:
Elizaveta Grushinskaya, world-famous Ballerina
Scullery Workers:
    Gunther Gustafsson
    Werner Holst
    Franz Kohl
    Ernst Schmidt
A Hotel Courtesan
Tootsie
Trude, a Maid
Detective

GRAND HOTEL — THE MUSICAL
SCENES AND MUSICAL NUMBERS

Prologue: the Presentation of the Company
"The Grand Parade"* ....The Company

Scene 1: The Lobby and Kitchen-Scullery
"Some Have, Some Have Not" ....Scullery Workers
"As It Should Be".. Baron Felix
"At The Grand Hotel*/Table With A View"............Kringelein

Scene 2: The Coffee Bar where The Jimmys entertain nightly
"Maybe My Baby Loves Me" ......The Jimmys & Flaemmchen

Scene 3: A corner of a Hotel Ballroom
"Fire and Ice"...Grushinskaya
"Villa On A Hill".. Raffaela

Scene 4: Near and In Ladies' Cloakroom
"I Want to Go to Hollywood"* ....Flaemmchen

Scene 5: In and Near Men's Washroom
"Everybody's Doing It"*.................................... Zinnowitz
"The Crooked Path".. Preysing

Scene 6: Felix's Bedroom
"As It Should Be"...Felix

Scene 7: The Yellow Pavilion
"Who Couldn't Dance With You?" ....(A) Flaemmchen/Felix
....(B) Kringelein/Flaemmchen

Scene 8: A Meeting Room in the Hotel
"The Crooked Path" (Reprise) ....Preysing/Zinnowitz

Scene 9: Backstage at the Ballet Theater
"No Encore"...Grushinskaya

Scene 10: The Financial Corner of the Hotel Lobby

Scene 11: Backstage at Ballet/Facade of the Hotel
"Fire and Ice"...Company

---

*by Maury Yeston

---

* by Maury Yeston

AUTHOR'S NOTE:

In writing the book of "GRAND HOTEL – The Musical," I worked from Vicki Baum's 1928 Novel, not the 1931 play or the 1933 MGM movie. The distinction is important as to tone and as to the ages of the major characters. For instance, Ms. Baum describes Baron Felix as 29, but John Barrymore was 52 when he played the part in the film. In the novel, Flaemmchen is described as 19; Grushinskaya as "old for a dancer whose career began when she was fifteen—perhaps forty-five." Kringelein, although terminally ill, is not old—Ms. Baum describes him as 47.

As to tone: In 1928 most people suffered from an excess of hope and optimism (illusions that few retained after the 1929 stock market crash, when play and movie were produced). Our Baron Felix, at least initially, believes that he'll make a killing in the stock market and pay off all his debts; Flaemmchen has little doubt that she can get the money she needs without prostituting herself. Preysing believes that a timely merger will save his company; Kringelein hopes that being in Grand Hotel will make his life of drudgery worthwhile.

Unlike in novel, play, or film, our characters are morally virgins at the outset. Felix owes but hasn't stolen; Preysing has never defrauded his stockholders. Flaemmchen knows in her heart that there's a good chance she's not pregnant—and why shouldn't she hope for a film career? In actuality, only two years earlier, Marlene Dietrich was spotted for her first theater job while sipping tea in one of the restaurants in the Adlon—Ms. Baum's model for her Grand Hotel.

Finally, I doubt very much if there were any Nazis in Ms. Baum's mind when she wrote the novel. The scullery workers in the musical are angry because they're not getting in on the action. When the crash comes, some of them might become Nazis, but some might become Communists—or perhaps they'll all hear about a "hot, hot stock," and move upstairs as hotel guests. In 1928, people believed in things like that—unlike today?

Luther Davis

GRAND HOTEL – The Musical

SCENE: The entire action takes place in Grand Hotel, Berlin — the world's most expensive hotel. Built at the beginning of the twentieth century, it is solid and sumptuous, perhaps a trifle faded, but never frayed.

TIME: 1928 — midway between the World Wars, the height of the stock-market boom, when Berlin was regarded as one of the world's great centers of high life.

NOTE: *Grand Hotel – The Musical* is designed to be performed continuously without intermission in a unit set into which occasional pieces of furniture can be moved by people in hotel livery. Scenes have been numbered for reference only — action (and almost all the music) is continuous.

The cast remains onstage throughout the show, sitting around the perimeter in semi-darkness and serving as singing chorus from time to time.

All the characters are assumed to be speaking German throughout (except when another language is specified). Thus there should be no Germanisms such as "Guten Morgen," "Mein Herr," or "Dankeshoen."

Audiences should be advised in advance that there will not be an intermission.

While there is no overture, the original Broadway production began with a tall doorman taking his post, standing at attention before the revolving door. Then there was heard a somewhat stylized tuning-up sound from the orchestra, and then, on tape, dimly heard, a mixture of hotel lobby sounds: talking, faintly heard bells, female laughter.

Then came the Prologue:

PROLOGUE

We hear more distinct sounds of Grand Hotel: ding-dings of BELLS ... the hotel TELEPHONE OPERATORS. Most VOICES overlap:

(BELL.)

TELEPHONE OPERATOR #1. Grand Hotel Berlin, good morning. [etc.]

(BELL.)

TELEPHONE OPERATOR #2. Grand Hotel, at your service. [etc.]

(BELL. The revolving door is on a pedestal which is free-standing. DOORMAN begins to push it to Up Center.)

TELEPHONE OPERATOR #3. Grand Hotel Berlin, at your service. [etc.]

(Music Cue # 1/1A: GRAND PARADE)

VOICE #1. Hello, would you send up a porter? Prepare my bill, please. [etc.]
VOICE #2. Hello, operator? Ice water to room 414. [etc.]
VOICE #3. Front desk? Have my car sent around in twenty minutes. [etc.]
VOICE #4. Hello, room service? His Excellency would like a champagne breakfast for two. [etc.]
VOICE #5. Front desk, I need the hairdresser right away. Yes, the hairdresser. [etc.]

15

VOICE #6. Hello, this is Mister Jannings in room three-twelve. I'd like another apartment, please. [etc.]

VOICE #7. Hello, operator, this is room two three seven. Send floor valet right away! [etc.]

VOICE #8. Operator, are there any messages for me? [etc.]

VOICE #9. Cab for Prince Obolensky! Cab for Prince Obolensky! Cab for Prince Obolensky! [etc.]

(These sounds grow and overlap ... among them we hear a premonitory DRONE which culminates in music. MUSIC CUE lA.
LIGHTS come up on a portion of the stage which might well be a corner of a bedroom in the hotel. The DOCTOR enters, or is discovered. HE is in great pain. HE was a Colonel in the German Army Medical Corps, 1914-18 and was badly wounded. HE has lost an eye; one leg is nearly useless. HE fumbles urgently in his medical bag and brings out a hypodermic syringe. HE injects himself with what we will discover is morphine. The underscoring becomes calmer, and richer. Relieved, relaxed, HE turns toward the audience and gestures as if introducing us to the hotel:
LIGHTS come up. A dancing couple [GIGOLO and COUNTESS] glides across the lobby.
The GRAND PARADE begins as the revolving door, now Upstage, begins to turn. The CHARACTERS IN THE PLAY enter one by one through the door, come Downstage, bow, and take seats on small gilt chairs.
THEY sing "THE GRAND PARADE.")

DOCTOR.	COMPANY.
VELVET STAIRS,	AH's
EASY CHAIRS,	
PERFUMED AIR	
GENTLY BLOWING.	

CHANDELIERS—

LIGHT APPEARS
BURNING BRIGHT,
  CRYSTAL GLOWING.

PEOPLE COME, PEOPLE
  GO,
WAVE OF LIFE
  OVERFLOWING!
COME, BEGIN
IN OLD BERLIN,
YOU'RE IN
THE GRAND HOTEL!
  ALL.
GRAND HOTEL!
GRAND HOTEL!
MUSIC CONSTANTLY
  PLAYING!

GRAND HOTEL!
LIVING WELL
WHERE THE WEALTHY
  ARE STAYING!

ROUND AND ROUND,
HEAR THE SOUND,
HEAR WHAT PEOPLE
  ARE SAYING!

IT'S THE DIN
OF OLD BERLIN,
YOU'RE IN THE
  GRAND HOTEL!

GROUP #1.	**GROUP #2.**
VELVET STAIRS,	AT THE GRAND,
EASY CHAIRS,	YOU ARE AT THE
	GRAND!
PERFUMED AIR	AT THE GRAND,
GENTLY BLOWING.	

CHANDELIERS—   YOU ARE AT THE
                            GRAND!
LIGHT APPEARS   AT THE GRAND
BURNING BRIGHT,   HOTEL! [etc.]
  CRYSTAL GLOWING.

IN THEY COME, OUT
  THEY GO,
  ALL.
WAVE OF LIFE OVERFLOWING!
COME, BEGIN IN OLD BERLIN,
YOU'RE IN THE GRAND HOTEL!

DOCTOR. Grand Hotel, Berlin. Always the same. People come. People go. Look at them—living the high life! But time is running out. (*Introducing them.*) The great Grushinskaya—the fabled ballerina making a farewell tour. Her eighth.

Raffaela—her devoted companion.

Hermann Preysing—a businessman reporting to his stockholders.

Miss Frieda Flamm—a typist. (*Adds, as FLAEMMCHEN shows a lot of leg.*) But not for long.

Otto Kringelein, a bookkeeper looking for "Life"!

The famous ladies' man, Baron Felix Amadeus Benvenuto von Gaigern, heir to a small title—and large debts.

(CHAUFFEUR enters and speaks to Baron.)

CHAUFFEUR. My boss wants payment now.

BARON. Don't talk to me in public with a cigarette in your mouth.

CHAUFFEUR. My boss always gets what he wants.

BARON. I'm busy.

CHAUFFEUR. Doing what?

BARON. Breathing. *(BARON walks away.)*

DOCTOR. There's nothing more useless on this planet than a nobleman without money.
COMPANY.
COME, BEGIN IN OLD BERLIN,
YOU'RE IN THE GRAND HOTEL!

(MUSIC changes and takes on an angry beat ... The LIGHTING changes and SEVERAL KITCHEN/ SCULLERY WORKERS appear carrying dirty dishes in wire baskets. Indications are that They're in a backstairs area—perhaps They're surrounded by clouds of STEAM.)

(Music Cue #1B: OPENING PART II)

SCENE 1

The Scullery and the Lobby.

SCULLERY WORKERS.
SOME HAVE, SOME HAVE NOT!
SOME HAVE, SOME HAVE NOT!
SOME HAVE, SOME HAVE NOT!
SCULLERY #1.
GOD! HEAVIER EVERY DAY!
SCULLERY #2.
BUSINESS MUST BE GOOD.
SCULLERY #1.
THEY'RE RAKING IT IN, ALL OF THEM UP
THERE!
SCULLERY #3.
ALL OF THEM UP THERE!
SCULLERY #4.
DIRTY WORK!

SCULLERY WORKERS.
EVERY BUM AND BITCH IN ALL BERLIN IS RICH
  EXCEPT FOR US!

(MUSIC CUE #lB)

THE HOTEL STAFF. (*Joining.*)
SOME HAVE, SOME HAVE NOT! WHY?
THEY'RE IN HERE SPENDING MONEY:
A MILLION MARKS A DAY!
WE'RE ONE STEP FROM THE STREET,
MAKING JUST ENOUGH TO EAT
FOR A DAY,
WEEK,
MONTH,
YEAR …
WITH A THOUSAND BILLS TO PAY!
THEY HAVE US RUN TO HAIL THEIR CABS
WHILE THEY'RE RUNNING UP THEIR TABS,
DRINKING MAGNUMS OF CHAMPAGNE!
AND WE PRAY FOR TIPS OF A MARK,
FRANC,
DOLLAR,
POUND!
MADAME PEEPEE.
I'D
LIKE TO OCCUPY A ROYAL SUITE
INSTEAD OF MOPPING FLOORS
WHERE THE WHORES
TRACK MUD AND CRUD PAST THE BELLHOPS!

(SHE snorts, continues pushing broom.)

BARON.
GIVE ME THE THRILL
OF A CARELESS
  EXISTENCE!
GIVE ME THE HEAT

AND THE PASSION TO
  WIN!
I WANT THE HEIGHT
AND ROMANCE OF
  ADVENTURE,
COOLED BY THE CHILL
OF THE DANGER I'M   **SCULLERY**
  IN!   **WORKERS.**
MY LIFE MUST BE A   THEY HAVE US RUN
  HOUSE OF CARDS   TO HAIL
                         THEIR CABS, WHILE
                           THEY'RE
                         RUNNING UP THEIR
                           TABS
GETTING HIGHER AND   DRINKING MAGNUMS
  HIGHER!   OF CHAMPAGNE!

A STEP ACROSS AN   THERE STANDS A MAN
  ENDLESS SPACE,
                         WHO'S MADE HIS
                           GOAL.
A DARING WALK ON A   I WOULD GIVE MY
  WIRE,   BONES
                         AND MY SOUL!

EACH DAY LIVED ON
  FIRE!
                         I WANT THAT
                           FELLOW'S
                           BANKROLL!
LET ME BE FREE   SOME HAVE, SOME
                           HAVE NOT!
                         GUNTHER
                         GUSTAFSSON.
TO BE ALL THAT I   *WHY*?
  COULD BE!

(MUSIC CUE # 1C: OPENING PART III)

TELEPHONE OPERATORS. (*Speak.*) Grand Hotel, at your service, [etc.]

ERIK. Good morning, Front Desk—Yes, this is Erik Litnauer—Is that you, nurse? What's happening at the hospital?—How is my wife?—Isn't the baby here yet?—Patience??? You can talk!—My wife's asking for me? She must know I can't get away. I'd lose my job. Is she still suffering very much?—What? I can't hear you!—(*HE breaks off as ROHNA cruises by, ends conversation by whispering.*) I'll come soon as I can! (*Hangs up.*)

COMPANY. GRAND HOTEL BERLIN!

(*GRUSHINSKAYA, WITT, SANDOR enter through revolving door. THEY are in mid-argument.*)

GRUSHINSKAYA. I cannot dance tonight! I will never dance again! (*SHE comes Downstage.*) How many times have I said that?

WITT. Hundreds, Madame. It is a small affliction, like sneezing.

GRUSHINSKAYA. Well, this time I mean it! *Grushinskaya est fini!* Cancel!

SANDOR. My God, Madame! All is in readiness for a triumphant opening tonight! You *must* dance! You have a contract! We have sold tickets!

GRUSHINSKAYA. Cancel!

WITT. Dear one—*cherie*—

GRUSHINSKAYA. *Qu'est-ce tu as? Qu'est-ce que tu veut?*

WITT. Is this you? You never disappoint people.

GRUSHINSKAYA. I would rather disappoint them than cheat them. I cannot dance any more! Grushinskaya retires!

WITT. *Mais ce n'est pas possible enfin, voyons!*

GRUSHINSKAYA. *Je ne peux plus rien faire!* Cancel!

SANDOR. I cannot allow you to cancel at this late hour. We've sold tickets.

GRUSHINSKAYA. What did he say? Is he speaking Hungarian? His accent is terrible.

ROHNA. *(Presenting a bouquet.)* Madame Grushinskaya, welcome to Grand Hotel.

(ROHNA hands GRUSHINSKAYA the flowers.)

GRUSHINSKAYA. *Merci beaucoup.* I am fond of your hotel, very fond, after so many visits—

SANDOR. *(Aside to Witt as THEY go.)* She cannot cancel so late! We have sold tickets!

WITT. We had a bad engagement in Amsterdam. No business, very bad press. Also, she stumbled on stage. An accident, no more, but she feels she's failed her audience ...

SANDOR. She absolutely must ...

RAFFAELA. *Basta!—Stiazitto!*

SANDOR. What did she say?

WITT. That's Italian.

GRUSHINSKAYA. I cannot believe that among the five of us we cannot find one language we all understand.

ROHNA. Excuse me. *Excusez moi. Scusi.*

RAFFAELA. *Silencio!*

ROHNA. Thank you! *(HE goes.)*

RAFFAELA. You must not press her about tonight—Madame is very tired!

GRUSHINSKAYA. Tired? I am completely exhaust! Victor, please pay off the company! Be generous—the orchestra, the dancers, everybody.

WITT. But, *cherie*—pay? With what?

GRUSHINSKAYA. You will have money tomorrow! Ample money! I promise!

ROHNA. Madame, may I show you to your apartment? Madame—

(As GRUSHINSKAYA and PARTY exit, SHE comes face-to-face with the BARON. Their eyes lock, then SHE goes.)

BARON. Ahh! Grushinskaya! Herself!
ROHNA. She always stays at Grand Hotel.
BARON. I've seen her dance. What grace!
ROHNA. May I respectfully remind the baron that his bill is six months in arrears?
BARON. Seven.

(HE turns away and takes out his gold cigarette case. ERIK steps forward with a lighter.)

BARON. Hello, Erik.
ERIK. Good morning, sir. *(Admiring the cigarette case reverently.)* It's such a handsome case, sir. It's sort of famous in the hotel. Are those diamonds?
BARON. So I have been told. It was my father's.
ERIK. Baron, sir—my wife was really—well, sort of overcome by the flowers. She'll write you as soon as it's over. Thank you, sir.
BARON. Baby not here yet? How is she?
ERIK. Pain!—how can women stand it!
BARON. It'll be all right. She's young and healthy—
CHAUFFEUR. *(Entering.)* Baron ...
BARON. Are you still here?
CHAUFFEUR. My employer is on the telephone. He wants to talk to you. That telephone booth over there.
BARON. Not now. Tell him I'll pay him when I can.
CHAUFFEUR. You know he's Algerian. He talks a lot about having your balls cut off.
BARON. Come to think of it, I *can* spare a moment.

(CHAUFFEUR leads the way to the telephone booth.)

OPERATORS/BELLBOYS. GRAND HOTEL AT YOUR SERVICE! [etc.] (*THEY continue as the BARON speaks.*)

BARON. (*Into telephone.*) Hello, I'll be able to pay you back in full—but to do so I'd have to borrow five thousand more—Why?—I have a tip on a stock on the New York Stock Exchange! Hello? (*Continuing to a dead phone.*)—a hot, hot stock which is sure to go right through the roof! (*Sings.*)
DANGEROUS GAME
AND A CARELESS EXISTENCE,
ONLY FOR THOSE
WITH THE COURAGE TO PLAY ...
AND THE MONEY TO PAY!

(*FLAEMMCHEN is seen in another booth.*)

(MUSIC CUE # 1D: OPENING PART IV)

FLAEMMCHEN. (*Into telephone.*) Hello! It's me! Frieda ... when did you get back? ... Oh, I'm at The Grand Hotel on a secretarial call. Listen, remember how you used to call me your "little flame"? Well, I'm going to steal that for a stage name: FLAEMMCHEN! That's going to be me! Just Flaemmchen, no last name. There's something so modern, so 1928 about it! Yes, it's for when I become a movie star! Garbo is *just* Garbo—never Greta!

PREYSING. (*Another booth.*) Operator, I'm expecting a radiogram from America. This is Mister Preysing, General Director Preysing of Saxonia Mills, I'm just checking in ... No radiogram? ... Very well. I wish to call Fredersdorf ... it's in Saxonia. The number is Fredersdorf 32.

RAFFAELA. (*Another booth.*) Pronto, Maison Cartier? I am calling for Madame Grushinskaya ... *Grushinskaya ... La prima ballerina del mondo!* ... Yes, the toe dancer. Madame wishes to sell some jewelry she has tired of.

KRINGELEIN. (*In another booth.*) Hello.

RAFFAELA. It is an extremely important piece of jewelry! Please put me through to your chief appraiser.

KRINGELEIN. Fredersdorf Hospital? My name is Kringelein, Otto ... ... Kringelein! I was in Cardiology Ward till last night. May I speak directly, and quickly, to Doctor Kampmann, please? ...

FLAEMMCHEN. YOU CALLED ME YOUR "LITTLE FLAME":

FLAEMMCHEN. Well, I thought we might have a Charleston or two or three ... All right then. I'll spill it on the phone. I need some money because, you see, I'm late ... *Late!* Only a couple of weeks, but usually I'm Miss Swiss Watch!

RAFFAELA. *ASPETTANDO.*

KRINGELEIN. QUICKLY!

RAFFAELA. *BUON GIORNIO, SIGNORE ...*

KRINGELEIN. I HAVEN'T MUCH TIME.

RAFFAELA. *SI, SI, CAPISCO.*

PREYSING. Mopsy—hello, my little darling—Yes, it's Daddy, all the way from Berlin—No, dear, it's too expensive to tell you stories on long distance—All right : the big, black crow went CAW! CAW! CAW! Now put Mommy on the phone—Hello,

Helga? I'm at the hotel—
No, no radiogram from
Boston, not yet—Of
course I'm upset! If we
don't get the Boston
merger our company's
down the drain! Time is
running out!

KRINGELEIN.
QUICKLY.
THIS WAITING,
IT COSTS SO MUCH
    MONEY!

FLAEMMCHEN.
I'M LATE!
I'M LATE! AH!
    KRINGELEIN.
THIS WAITING—
AND I'VE SO LITTLE
    TIME!

RAFFAELA.
LA COLLANA DI
    RUBIES!
LA COLLANA DI
    RUBIES!
DEVE RIMANERE SUA!

KRINGELEIN.
    Doctor Kampmann? It's
Otto Kringelein ... No,
I'm in Berlin ... Yes, I
saw the specialist. The
news is very, very bad ...
No, I'm not coming back
to hospital ... not ever.
Send my records to me
here ... my address? My
address from now on is:

PREYSING.
YES, I MISS YOU!

FLAEMMCHEN.
LET'S GET TOGETHER!
    PREYSING.
YES, I WISH I WERE
    HOME!
YES, YES, YES!

FLAEMMCHEN.
I WANT TO GO
TO HOLLYWOOD!

KRINGELEIN and **COMPANY.** GRAND
HOTEL BERLIN!

BARON. Hello, Mister Meehan? It's Baron von Gaigern. I need a little more time before I buy that stock. Yes, I understand. Time is running out.

FLAEMMCHEN. No! Women don't catch cold down there. All we catch down there is pregnant!

RAFFAELA. No. Madame does not go to stores. Stores come to her ... *Si,* today! Time is running out.

KRINGELEIN. It's the most expensive hotel in Europe. Even my old boss, Mister Preysing, is staying here.

PREYSING. ... Helga! No! There is no such word! Not for us! Not for the Preysing family is there such a word as *bankruptcy!*

FLAEMMCHEN. Look, please send the money ... No, it can't wait—Time is running out!

BARON. ... well, I'm trying to find a partner. Tell me, would you pay a *finder's fee* if I bring in a buyer—?

KRINGELEIN. I cashed in my savings, *everything!* Time is running out.

(All the following lines overlap.)

PREYSING. Don't cry. I'm going to solve this.

KRINGELEIN. I must talk quickly. It costs two-marks-ninety a minute.

PREYSING. Kiss our darling girls for me and, well...

FLAEMMCHEN. Thanks!

PREYSING. —pray for me here in the lion's den!

FLAEMMCHEN. Thanks for nothing at all!

KRINGELEIN. What? ... I've been sensible all my life!

BARON. You don't do that, eh? I see.

KRINGELEIN. Enough sensible. Bye-bye, Doctor.

BARON. So I have twenty-four hours.

RAFFAELA. *Va bene. A presto.*

BARON. I see.

PREYSING. Bye-bye, Helga!

KRINGELEIN. Bye-bye, Fredersdorf.

(MUSIC CUE #1E: OPENING PART V [CODA])

BARON.
OH FOR THE THRILL
OF A CARELESS
  EXISTENCE:
LIVE AS I WILL,

NO REGARD FOR THE
  FEE!

SINGERS.
SOME HAVE, SOME
  HAVE NOT!
SOME HAVE, SOME
  HAVE NOT!

I WANT TO LIVE IN
  LOVE AND RAGE
AND PLUCK THE
  FRUIT FROM THE
  VINE!

SCULLERIES &
BELLMEN.
EV'RY BUM AND
  BITCH IN BERLIN IS
  GETTING RICH
  EXCEPT FOR US!
  MME. PEEPEE.
I'D LIKE TO OCCUPY
  THE ROYAL SUITE
  [etc.]

I WANT TO GLITTER
  WITH THE AGE

AND DRINK EACH
  EXQUISITE WINE!
OH THAT LIFE MUST
  BE MINE!

OPERATORS &
SCULLERIES.
(*Simultaneously.*)
GRAND HOTEL AT
  YOUR SERVICE!
I WANT THAT
  FELLOW'S
  BANKROLL!
SCULLERIES &
PEEPEE.

LET ME WALK TALL

SOME HAVE, SOME
  HAVE NOT!

AND BE ALL THAT I
   COULD BE!

NEVER TO FALL,

EVER UP, NEVER
   DOWN!

AT THE TOP OF THE
   TOWN!

SOME HAVE, SOME
   HAVE NOT!
IF ONLY I WERE
   SMARTER
I WOULDN'T HAVE TO
   SWEAT SO MUCH!
TO HAVE THAT
   FELLOW'S
   BANKROLL
I COULD WHEEL AND
   DEAL,
CHEAT, STEAL,
   WHATEVER
HE DID TO GET SO
   MUCH!
IT'S THE DIN OF OLD
   BERLIN,
IT'S THE DIN OF OLD
   BERLIN,

ALL.
IT'S THE DIN OF OLD BERLIN:
YOU'RE IN THE GRAND HOTEL!

(By this point, in the 1989-92 Broadway production, the ENTIRE CAST had come all the way Downstage, singing straight out to the audience. At the pause here in the orchestration ALL IN THE CAST bowed— making this the first place where the dynamics of the show allowed applause.)

(MUSIC CUE # 2: TABLE WITH A VIEW)

ERIK. (*Approaching the Doctor.*) Perhaps the doctor would like to go to the ballet? There are good seats available for Grushinskaya.
DOCTOR. So Grushinskaya doesn't sell out anymore? I'm not surprised. She's still doing dances

about dying swans in an age where an entire generation of young men was wiped out—no, thanks.

ERIK. Colonel-Doctor—please, I ask your help. I talked to the hospital—my wife is in terrible pain.

DOCTOR. Pain? They call that pain? What does anyone know about pain who hasn't met mustard gas and shrapnel?

ERIK. People say you could prescribe medicine that kills pain.

DOCTOR. Don't be a fool! Morphine is for field hospitals, not maternity wards. It would harm the baby. Go hold her hand.

ERIK. Oh, I wish I could—but I have to be here. We need this job! God, how we need it!

(DOCTOR nods and ERIK goes Off.)

DOCTOR. Poor women, what a price they pay. *(To a reigning BEAUTY as SHE passes—but not so SHE can hear.)* Hold your head high while you can, you arrogant bitch! *(Beckons to BELLMAN, who approaches.)* See if there's any mail for me. Or messages. And tell Reception I *may* be checking out today.

BELLMAN. Sir, you said that yesterday.

(The DOCTOR gives him a sharp look and HE exits. KRINGELEIN comes in carrying all his worldly belongings. ROHNA sees him and gestures for BELLMAN to get the poor fellow out of there.)

KRINGELEIN. Please, I have a reservation! Please! I'm going to be a guest at Grand Hotel! My name is Kringelein, Otto Kringelein—

ROHNA. I'm afraid there isn't a thing today.

KRINGELEIN. But I have a reservation. If you check your book you'll see. The name is Kringelein, Otto.

ROHNA. Having a reservation is not the same as having a room. The house is full. There are hotels near the railway station. (*HE gestures to a BELLMAN who starts to carry out Kringelein's bags.*)

KRINGELEIN. No—please—please—you don't understand—Young man, those are my things! (*HE falls. ERIK catches him, places him in chair.*)

KRINGELEIN. (*Sings.*)
DON'T HOLD ME BACK,
DON'T TIE ME DOWN,
JUST LET MY FEET ROAM FREE!

DOCTOR. (*Approaches.*) I'm a doctor. Be quiet. Take deep breaths ... have you been in hospital? (*Taking his pulse.*)

KRINGELEIN. I left.

DOCTOR. What did they tell you?

KRINGELEIN. That I don't have long to live. Doctor, tell them, make them understand. I *have* to stay here!

DOCTOR. Here? Why, for God's sake?

KRINGELEIN. Life! Don't you see? It went by while I wasn't looking. I quite entirely missed it!

DOCTOR. You expect to find "Life" at Grand Hotel?

KRINGELEIN. Yes.

DOCTOR. Sir, "Life" is not a streetcar you can run after and catch. Nor does it reside here.

ERIK. Shall I call for an ambulance?

KRINGELEIN. No!

DOCTOR. No, he's all right. For the moment.

KRINGELEIN. Yes, I'm feeling much, much better. Thank you, Doctor.

DOCTOR. (*To Erik, as HE walks away.*) Tell Reception—I'll stay. One more day.

KRINGELEIN. (*To Erik.*) Please, young man ... I don't have these spells very often. Really, they're extremely rare. Please tell me: I see people leaving with their bags. Why is it you have no room for *me*? It is possible Grand Hotel does not take Jews?

ROHNA. (*Overhearing, HE hurries closer to say:*) Nonsense! I assure you, Baron Rothschild is even now upstairs in the Prince Albert Suite.

KRINGELEIN. Sir, when you have millions of marks you're maybe not so Jewish anymore. (*Sings.*)
SO HERE'S THE PLACE WHERE THE GREAT ONES
   WALK!
SO HERE'S THE PLACE WHERE THE SMART ONES
   TALK!
HERE'S WHERE THE GRAND ONES DINE ...

BARON. (*Coming over.*) Excuse me—(*To Rohna.*) Baron Rothschild's an old friend of my family's. Would it be helpful if I were to ask him to intercede for this gentleman?

ROHNA. (*Shocked.*) No! Do not disturb the baron, Baron.

KRINGELEIN. You, you're a baron? You see? I was right about Grand Hotel! Already I've met my first baron and I'm only in the lobby!

BARON. (*To Rohna.*) I really think I should call him.

ROHNA. Perhaps I could check the register one more time. (*Goes.*)

BARON. Yes, perhaps you could. (*To Kringlein.*) Hasn't anyone warned you that everything here costs double?

KRINGELEIN. (*Producing a bulging wallet.*) I don't have to worry about money anymore.

BARON. Ah, I see! Made your pile, now wine and women?

KRINGELEIN. Wine and women? Baron, sir, I don't even have a room!

BARON. I'll just go see how he's doing. (*The BARON crosses to join Rohna.*)

(MUSIC CUE #2A: AT THE GRAND HOTEL)

DOCTOR. Look at him—He's dying and he wants to live. I'm living and can't wait to die.

KRINGELEIN. *(Sings.)*
FROM THE HOSPITAL
TO THE TOWN OF BERLIN,
I HAVE TAKEN THE TRAIN HERE
TO BEGIN
MY NEW LIFE,
THOUGH QUITE SOON THAT MUST END!
BUT UNTIL THAT OCCURS
I DO INTEND TO REMAIN.
I WANT TO KNOW THAT I ONCE WAS HERE
WHILE ALL MY FACULTIES STILL ARE CLEAR,

AND CHECK INTO MY ROOM,
AS I'VE PLANNED,
AT THE GRAND HOTEL!

I WANT TO SIT WHERE I CAN SIT
AND STARE LIFE IN THE EYE!
I WANT TO GO TO THE GRAND CAFE,
WHERE LIFE BEGINS AT THE END OF DAY,
AND HAVE THEM SHOW ME TO
A LITTLE TABLE WITH A VIEW!

THE SLEEK YOUNG MEN,
THE SLENDER GIRLS,
THEY PLEASE MY EYES!
PERFUMES FROM FRANCE
AND TROPIC PLANTS
AROUND ME RISE!

I LISTEN TO THE SWISH OF THE SILK AND
THE TUNE THE FIDDLE PLAYS,
AND I FEEL YOUNG AND WARM AND FREE!

THIS IS "DAS LEBEN"!
THIS IS "LA VITA"!

THIS IS "LA VIE,"
THE LIFE FOR ME!

(The BARON crosses to Kringelein, a room key in his hand.)

BARON. What luck! Room 418 is available. I believe it's one of their very best. (*HE hands him the key.*) Welcome to Grand Hotel, Old Socks.
KRINGELEIN. (*Overwhelmed.*) Thank you, may I say "friend"?
BARON. Of course.
ERIK. Right this way, sir. (*HE follows Kringelein's baggage out.*)
KRINGELEIN.
IN THIS LOBBY,
PAST THESE GOLD-COVERED WALLS,
PAST THE TAPESTRIES HANGING,
I'LL WALK MILES OF HALLS!
I WANT TO KNOW THAT I ONCE WAS HERE
WHILE ALL MY FACULTIES STILL WERE CLEAR:
I BROKE OUT OF MY SHELL ...
TO LIVE SWELL ...

(Grand pause.)

AT THE GRAND HOTEL ...

(Pause; cough; almost silently.)

AT THE GRAND HOTEL.

(Tosses key in the air and starts Off
At this point in the Broadway production there was a slight pause in the dynamics of the show, allowing applause.)

SCENE 2

(MUSIC CUE #3: MAYBE MY BABY)

The Coffee Bar.
*Two Black American entertainers, THE JIMMYS, have
entered and now begin setting up a bar. THEY are
rehearsing; THEY sing as THREE TELEPHONE
OPERATORS appreciate them.*

THE JIMMYS.
SHA DOOT- 'N BAH DUM DOO DAY,
SHA DOOT- 'N BAH DUM DOO DAY,
SHA DOOT- 'N BAH DUM DOO DAY,
SHA DOOT- 'N BAH DOOM!

SHA DOOT- 'N BAH DUM DOO DAY,
SHA DOOT- 'N BAH DUM DOO DAY,
SHA DOOT- 'N BAH DUM DOO DAY,
SHA DOOT- 'N BAH DUM DOO DAY,
SHA DOOT- 'N BAH DUM DOO DAY,
SHA DOOT- 'N BAH DUM DOO DAY,
SHA DOOT- 'N BAH DOOM!

SHA DOOT- 'N BAH DUM DOO DAY,
SHA DOOT- 'N BAH DUM DOO DAY,
SHA DOOT- 'N BAH DUM DOO DAY!

*(During this, FLAEMMCHEN enters and, in pantomime,
picks up house telephone.)*

FLAEMMCHEN. Operator, General Director
Preysing's room, please—Well, tell him the typist he
ordered is waiting downstairs—(*Looks around.*)—at the
coffee bar. (*SHE hangs up and approaches the bar.*)
JIMMY #2. (*Admiring the Phone Operators.*) *Tu as
vu,* Jimmy?

JIMMY #1. *J'ai vu*, Jimmy, *j'ai vu*!
JIMMY #2. *Qui prefers-tu*, Jimmy?
JIMMY #1. *Toutes les trois*, Jimmy—*toutes les trois*!
THE JIMMYS. (*THEY sing.*)
MAYBE MY BABY LOVES ME,
LOVES ME, LOVES ME,
BUT IF MY BABY LOVES ME
WHY DOES SHE TREAT ME SO MEAN?

MAYBE MY BABY WANTS ME,
NEEDS ME, CRAVES ME,
BUT IF MY BABY CRAVES ME
WHY AM I LOOKIN' SO LEAN?
   JIMMY #1.   **JIMMY #2.**
I CAN'T SLEEP NIGHTS BOOM, BOOM ...
WOND'RING WHERE
  SHE IS,
WITH WHOM SHE IS,
FOR WHAT!
                         I WORRY A LOT!
  BOTH JIMMYS.
MAYBE MY BABY LOVES ME,
BUT OH, IF SO,
WHY DOES MY BABY LEAVE ME
CRYIN' ALONE IN MY COT?
MAYBE MY LOVIN' BABY
LOVES ME NOT!
  SHA-DIDDLEY DOO BOP DOO BOP'N DOO BAY,
  SHA-DIDDLEY DOO BOP DOO BOP'N DOO BAY,
  SHA-DIDDLEY DOO BOP DOO BOP'N DOO BAY,
  SHA-DIDDLEY DOO BOP,
  SHA-DIDDLEY DOO BOP,
  SHA-DIDDLEY DOO BOP,
  SHA-DIDDLEY DOO BOP'N DOO BAY,
  SHA-DIDDLEY DOO BOP DOO BOP'N DOO BAY,
  SHA-DIDDLEY DOO BOP DOO BOP'N DOO BAY,
  SHA-DIDDLEY DOO BOP,
  SHA-DIDDLEY DOO BOP,

SHA-DIDDLEY DOO BOP,
SHA-DIDDLEY DOO BOP,
SHA-DIDDLEY DOO BOP—

FLAEMMCHEN. Is that le Jazz hot?

JIMMY #2. It will be after a few more rehearsals.

FLAEMMCHEN. You're rehearsing?

JIMMY #1. For the cabaret show tonight. *Je m'appelle Jimmy.*

JIMMY #2. *Je m'appelle Jimmy aussi!*

BOTH JIMMYS. *Et toi?*

FLAEMMCHEN. Flaemmchen, no last name.

BOTH JIMMYS. Flaemmchen! Oh la la! *Seulement* Flaemmchen!

FLAEMMCHEN. Excuse me, but are you French?

JIMMY #2. Are you kidding? Strictly American.

JIMMY #1. South Carolina.

JIMMY #2. *North* Carolina.

BOTH JIMMYS. *Mais nous habitons ici maintenant!*

FLAEMMCHEN. Why do you speak French in Germany?

JIMMY #2. French? Was that French? *(Turning to Jimmy #1.)* I'm gonna kill the guy who sold us those German lessons!

JIMMY #1. Joke. We played Paris last month.

FLAEMMCHEN. Please—tell me about America. Is it really the land of opportunity?

JIMMY #1. *(To Jimmy #2.)* Opportunity? What's that?

FLAEMMCHEN. Are the streets really paved with gold?

JIMMY #2. Honey, where I come from they ain't even paved!

JIMMY #1. Flaemmchen—you're so pretty. *(With a wink to Jimmy #2.)* Has anyone ever told you you oughta be in pictures?

FLAEMMCHEN. Funny you should ask. I tell myself that all the time!

(THEY sing and dance together.)

THE JIMMYS and FLAEMMCHEN.
SHA-DIDDLEY DOO BOP
SHA-DIDDLEY DOO BOP
SHA-DIDDLEY DOO BOP
SHA-DIDDLEY DOO BOP
SHA-DIDDLEY DOO BOP

MAYBE MY BABY LOVES ME,
BUT OH, IF SO,
WHY DOES MY BABY LEAVE ME
CRYIN' ALONE IN MY COT?
MAYBE MY LOVIN' BABY LOVES ME,
MAYBE MY LOVIN' BABY LOVES ME,
MAYBE MY BABY LOVES ME-E-E-E-E—
NOT!

SCENE 3

(MUSIC CUE #4: AFTER MAYBE MY BABY)

A corner of a Ballroom.
GRUSHINSKAYA, in tutu and toe shoes, is warming up
as WITT and SANDOR stand by.

GRUSHINSKAYA. Victor! Don't get your hopes up, I'm just limbering.
WITT. *Cherie,* you know you have to dance tonight. We need money.
GRUSHINSKAYA. I have retire.
SANDOR. But they don't want you to retire, Madame! Just listen to what it says in the newspaper: "We will never willingly say farewell to the world's greatest prima ballerina! She is a dancer for the ages. She

is fire and ice: fire in the passion she brings to her roles, and—"

GRUSHINSKAYA and SANDOR. "—ice in her technical perfection—"

GRUSHINSKAYA.—You cannot fool me, Sandor, that's an *old* review! From my *last* farewell tour.

SANDOR. But it is still correct. "Fire and ice."

GRUSHINSKAYA. Well, the "fire" is dying and the "ice" is melting.

WITT. *Cherie!* I cannot let you talk this way!

GRUSHINSKAYA. Real fire and ice does not stumble on stage!

WITT. An accident!

GRUSHINSKAYA. There are too many accidents! Victor, look through my eyes—the world has grown old—You are old, Sandor is old—the theatres are old, the ballets are old—one must feel *young* to dance, and there is nothing in my life to make me feel young. Nothing. It's time to quit. I am not dancing tonight!

SANDOR. But the house is sold out to the top gallery! They stood in line all night! People slept in the street! The curtain *must* go up!

GRUSHINSKAYA. That's what understudies are for.

WITT. People do not pay thirty marks to see an understudy!

GRUSHINSKAYA. My understudy is very good.

SANDOR. No, she's not!

GRUSHINSKAYA. You're right. She's terrible. Oh, Victor—must I?

WITT. Yes. You must.

GRUSHINSKAYA. (*SHE sighs.*) Only for you, then. (*Offers her hand.*)

WITT. *Merci!* (*Kisses her hand.*) *Merci.*

SANDOR. Yes. Thank you, Madame. Come, Victor, we musn't be late for the orchestra rehearsal. (*MUSIC CUE #5 BEFORE FIRE AND ICE.*) Those goddamn musicians are costing a fortune!

WITT. Goodbye, *cherie.* You will dance like an angel!

GRUSHINSKAYA. I know. "Fire and ice."

(WITT and SANDOR exit her room.
GRUSHINSKAYA starts her barre. WITT and SANDOR go down the hall.)

WITT. I am so relieved that we have a full house! I'm so relieved! She needs it so much.

SANDOR. I can't even give away seats. I've tried.

WITT. (*Stops, horrified.*) That was all a lie? You lied to her?

SANDOR. A manager must manage. After this, no more ballet for me. Jazz. Only jazz. And nudity. Josephine Baker.

WITT. Oh, my poor Madame! When she sees another empty house—it will break her heart.

(WITT and SANDOR exit. RAFFAELA enters.)

RAFFAELA. I hear we are dancing tonight?

GRUSHINSKAYA. Trot out the old firehorse once more.

RAFFAELA. The jewelry appraiser was here. He's very interested in your beautiful necklace; very impressed. (*SHE takes fabulous necklace from a box in her purse.*) Dear Madame—I don't want you to sell it— (*SHE puts necklace around Grushinskaya's neck.*) It is all you have left from your handsome Grand Duke.

GRUSHINSKAYA. Grand Duke Sergei is dead. This is from another age—Just like me.

RAFFAELA. I remember the night he gave it to you. In St. Petersburg. He called it "frozen applause," for your beauty.

GRUSHINSKAYA. He was young. Young men say silly things like that. I was young too. I believed silly things like that. (*Examines the necklace.*) Do you think it will bring enough to pay everyone?

RAFFAELA. Madame, listen, I have saved a great deal of money. Let me help!

GRUSHINSKAYA. Dear Raffaela—how kind you are! I am glad you have saved your pennies. But absolutely not. Raffaela—why have you put up with me all these years? My tempers, my tears, my vanity, my thoughtlessness—even my laundry. I've asked so much and paid so little. Why, Raffaela?

RAFFAELA. Madame is a great artist.

GRUSHINSKAYA. *Was.* What is it you want?

RAFFAELA. Madame needs me.

GRUSHINSKAYA. But what do *you* need?

(A pause.)

RAFFAELA. I—need to fix the ribbons on your toe shoes or they won't be ready for tonight.

GRUSHINSKAYA. And I need to limber. *Grazie*, Raffaela. *Grazie.*

RAFFAELA. *Prego.* (*SHE goes.*)

(MUSIC CUE #5A: FIRE AND ICE)

GRUSHINSKAYA. (*Begins practicing.*) Pain, pain, pain! *Un deux trois.*

COMPANY.
"FIRE AND ICE,
PASSION AND SHEER PERFECTION
ON THE STAGE
FEARLESSLY FLYING!"
CHEERS ... BRAVOS ...
ALL OF THE CROWD ENCHANTED,
GRAND APPLAUSE,
LOVE NEVER DYING!

GRUSHINSKAYA.
WERE THOSE YEARS

WORTH ALL THAT I GAVE UP?
HOW WAS I TO SAVE UP
THE LIFE I LET GO
IN ORDER TO DANCE?
    COMPANY.
"FIRE AND ICE,
PASSION AND SHEER PERFECTION"
IN THE WINGS QUIETLY SIGHING ...

(In her own small room, RAFFAELA sings.)

(MUSIC CUE #5B: TWENTY-TWO YEARS)

RAFFAELA. Oh, dear Elizaveta—it is not pennies I have saved. For twenty-two years I have invested in stocks and bonds everything you ever paid me, waiting for the day when time would run out and you have no one to turn to but me. Twenty-two years—*(Sings.)*
FOR TWENTY-TWO YEARS
I HAVE KEPT SECRETS FROM YOU,
TWENTY-TWO YEARS
I'VE PROTECTED YOU
FROM THE HARSHNESS OF LIFE ...

ALWAYS FEELING FOR YOU
A KIND OF LOVE.

(MUSIC CUE #6: VILLA ON A HILL)

DEAR ONE,
COME WHERE THE VINES GROW,
COME, COME AND WE'LL FIND
A VILLA ON A HILL
IN POSITANO.

SOMEDAY
HIGH IN OUR ARBOR
FAR, FAR FROM TONIGHT,

WE'LL GAZE IN DELIGHT
DOWN ON THE HARBOR.

WHEN THOSE FABLED FEET
DANCE DOWN THAT ANCIENT STREET,
OH, THE THOUGHT OF THAT
IS SWEET, SWEET!
FAR FROM
BERLIN OR MILANO
I KNOW WE WILL FIND
TRUE PEACE OF MIND,
A PEACE THAT WILL FILL
OUR VILLA ON A HILL
IN POSITANO!
    GRUSHINSKAYA.
WERE THOSE YEARS
WORTH ALL THAT I GAVE UP?
    COMPANY.
"FIRE AND ICE!
FIRE AND ICE!"

(The BARON has passed and again his eyes fix on Grushinskaya before SHE turns and goes as FLAEMMCHEN crosses.)

SCENE 4

Near and in a Ladies' Cloakroom.
FLAEMMCHEN enters, pantomimes picking up the house telephone.

(MUSIC CUE #6A: BEFORE GIRL IN THE MIRROR)

FLAEMMCHEN. General Director Preysing's room, please—the line's still busy?—Well, please tell him the typewriting person he ordered is *still* waiting downstairs. Thank you.

(During this the BARON has passed, notices her and likes what HE sees; HE stays to admire. When SHE hangs up the phone and starts Off, HE follows her.)

BARON. Hello. There's a pretty new face.
FLAEMMCHEN. Yours isn't so bad yourself.
BARON. Sorry about your stocking—
FLAEMMCHEN. *(Looking.)* Damn! Twelve marks a pair! My typewriter must've snagged it.
BARON. Then you really are a typewriting person. With your looks?
FLAEMMCHEN. Well, that's the way I pay my rent. Of course, I'd rather be starring in films and eating caviar. You're not a film producer by any chance—?
BARON. Sorry.
FLAEMMCHEN. Me too.

(SHE heads into the ladies' room where TWO TOOTSIES are primping at the mirror, which is presumed to be Downstage.)

TOOTSIE #1. *(Leafing through several kinds of currency.)* Excuse me—how many marks to the English pound?
TOOTSIE #2. *(Eyes straight ahead.)* Eighteen, I think.
TOOTSIE #1. And the American dollar?
TOOTSIE #2. Four or five.
TOOTSIE #1. And the Swiss franc?
TOOTSIE #2. One for one.
TOOTSIE #1. Say! I had a pretty good night!

(The BARON has followed Flaemmchen into the ladies' room.)

BARON.—Did I hear you say you like caviar?

TOOTSIE #1. Really! The men's room is right next door!

BARON. I know. Haven't I seen you there?

(Affronted, SHE goes, her FRIEND only lingering to admire the Baron. The BARON smiles at Flaemmchen.)

BARON. Shall we say five o'clock this evening at the Yellow Pavilion?

FLAEMMCHEN. Good Lord, you've got a way with you! Good Lord!

BARON. They have a nifty new dance band. I'll wait for you there.

FLAEMMCHEN. Will you now? (*HE lights her cigarette.*)

FLAEMMCHEN. And you expect me to drop everything and look you up?

BARON. Yes, please.

FLAEMMCHEN. You could be a lot of trouble to a girl like me.

BARON. What sort of girl is that?

FLAEMMCHEN. Sometimes I do—dumb things.

BARON. Me too. Very dumb. Yellow Pavilion. Five o'clock. (*The BARON exits.*)

FLAEMMCHEN. (*Sings, looking into mirror.*)
WHAT DID HE SEE IN ME?
WHAT'S MY ATTRACTION?
COULD THAT FACE MAKE A MILLION MEN
   ADORE ME?
AND MAKE A HUNDRED CAMERAMEN EXPLORE
   ME?
IS THAT THE GIRL I SEE THERE RIGHT BEFORE
   ME?

(MUSIC CUE #6B: GIRL IN THE MIRROR)

I WANNA BE THAT GIRL IN THE MIRROR THERE!
I WANNA BE THAT GIRL WITH GOLDEN HAIR
UP ON A SILVER SCREEN
MOST EV'RYWHERE IN THE WORLD!

I WANT TO GO TO HOLLYWOOD!
TALKIES!
I MEAN THE PICTURES!
I WANNA HAVE A HOT TIME EV'RY NIGHT:
GET OUT AND RAISE A LITTLE FAHRENHEIT,
KNOCK EV'RY DUKE AND COUNT AND BARON.
   RIGHT OFF HIS FEET!
I'LL BE THAT GIRL, THAT'S UNDERSTOOD, OH!
I WANT TO GO TO HOLLYWOOD!

I WANNA SING THE BLUES,
I WANNA WEAR NICE SHOES,
AND DRINK ILLEGAL BOOZE
IN EV'RY LATE-NIGHT SPOT FOR "LE JAZZ HOT"!
I WANNA BREAKFAST, LUNCH AND DINNER
   THERE
IF I'M A BIG BOX-OFFICE WINNER THERE!
I'LL BE THE MOST WELL-KNOWN BERLINER
   THERE EVER WAS!
I WANT TO GO TO HOLLYWOOD,
SO I CAN GET FAR AWAY FROM—

FRIEDRICHSTRASSE:
MY COLD WATER FLAT,
THE SOFA THAT I SLEEP ON BEHIND THE
   SCREEN,
THE NOISY LODGER IN THE NEXT ROOM,
MY BROKEN HAND MIRROR,
MY BROKEN COFFEE POT!
IF THINGS GET BROKEN, THEY STAY BROKEN
IN FRIEDRICHSTRASSE!

THE WORN-OUT BRISTLES ON YOUR
    HAIRBRUSH,
THE PENNIES NEEDED FOR THE HEAT EV'RY
    HOUR,
AND WHEN YOU GET SICK YOU *STAY* SICK
IN FRIEDRICHSTRASSE,
WHERE YOU LIVE WITH LITTLE SOAP AND WITH
    HARDLY ANY HOPE!

I WANNA BE THAT GIRL IN THE MIRROR THERE!
I WANNA BE THAT GIRL WITH GOLDEN HAIR
UP ON A SILVER SCREEN
MOST EV'RYWHERE IN THE WORLD!

I WANT TO GO TO HOLLY—
I WANT TO GO, I WANT TO GO, I WANT TO GO,
I WANT TO GO, I WANT TO GO, I HAVE TO GO,
I HAVE TO GO, I HAVE TO GO, I HAVE TO GO!

I SWEAR THAT GIRL IN THE MIRROR,
THAT GIRL IN THE MIRROR,
IS GOING TO GO
TO HOLLYWOOD!
    FLAEMMCHEN & COMPANY.
HOLLYWOOD!
HOLLYWOOD!
HOLLYWOOD!
    FLAEMMCHEN. (*Spoken.*) Hollywood!

(Applause segue to:)

(MUSIC CUE #6C: EVERYBODY'S DOING IT)

SCENE 5

In and near the Men's Washroom.

PREYSING is walking through corridors with an angry attorney named ZINNOWITZ. THEY enter a washroom.

ZINNOWITZ. Your shareholders are angry.

PREYSING. I'm not worried.

ZINNOWITZ. I tell you they're ready to replace you as General Director. Unless you can produce a miracle. And the only miracle I know about is a merger with those Americans in Boston, Massachusetts.

PREYSING. The shareholders won't throw me out after so many profitable years. Why, when my wife's father was alive—

ZINNOWITZ. Those years are gone, Preysing! Is the Boston merger on or not?

PREYSING. (*Pantomimes washing his hands while looking in mirror.*) I'm not sure. I'm still waiting for a radiogram.

ZINNOWITZ. We've got to buy time. At the meeting today you'll have to tell them the merger is on.

PREYSING. You mean *lie* to them? My God, I couldn't do that!

ZINNOWITZ. Don't be a fool! (*Sings.*)
YOU WANT TO PUT A LOCK
ON THE COMPANY STOCK.
IT'S A BLOCK OF TWENTY THOUSAND—
YOU'RE ALREADY IN THE RED,
AND YOU WON'T TELL A LITTLE BITTY LIE
TO GET AHEAD?
EVERYBODY'S DOING IT ...
EVERYBODY'S DOING IT.

PREYSING. You shouldn't even suggest such a thing! You, a lawyer—

ZINNOWITZ. Oh, I forgot. You're the very model of an honest businessman.

PREYSING. Yes, I am!

ZINNOWITZ. Well, wake up, for God's sake! You've living in the dark ages! This is 1928! (*Sings.*)

LOOK AROUND HERE, LOOK AROUND THERE!
BREAK A LITTLE SECRET, MAKE A LITTLE
  SCARE,
MOVE A LITTLE STOCK!
WHO IS THERE TO CARE?
EVERYBODY'S DOING IT ...
EVERYBODY'S DOING IT!
  PREYSING. I have my reputation to uphold!
  ZINNOWITZ. Really.

(THEY leave the men's room.)

  PREYSING. Yes, really.
  ZINNOWITZ. How much of your wife's money have you poured into the company to stabilize the shares—two hundred thousand?
  PREYSING. Closer to three—
  ZINNOWITZ. God in Heaven, Preysing! You're out on the limb for three hundred thousand marks, and your job *and* you can't bring yourself to fib a little? *(Sings.)*
EVERYBODY OUT THERE
TRYING TO GET HIS—
SAYS IT'S REALLY BETTER
THAN HE KNOWS IT REALLY IS!
EVERYBODY'S DOING IT!
EVERYBODY'S DOING IT!
  PREYSING. Well, not me! Never!

(FLAEMMCHEN enters, carrying typewriter.)

  ZINNOWITZ. All right, Preysing, be Mister Honest...
  PREYSING. Yes, I will! Thank you! I have to live with myself—with my wife, my children!
  ZINNOWITZ. You'll lose everything, Preysing! *(Exits.)*

FLAEMMCHEN. Excuse me, you're Mister Preysing?

PREYSING. Yes, I'm General Director Preysing.

FLAEMMCHEN. You ordered a typist?

PREYSING. Yes.

FLAEMMCHEN. Then you ordered me.

PREYSING. Oh?

FLAEMMCHEN. My name is Flaemmchen. Just Flaemmchen.

PREYSING. Just Flaemmchen. Yes, I need to type some notes for a stockholders' meeting. I don't like to speak extemporaneously. Come along.

FLAEMMCHEN. I don't go to rooms.

PREYSING. Well, of course not. I have rented a conference office. Miss, I'm a married man!

FLAEMMCHEN. Oh. Then I have nothing to worry about.

(BELLMAN enters.)

BELLMAN. Radiogram for Mister Preysing ... Mister Preysing—

PREYSING. Preysing, that's me. Yes, yes! Some important information I've been waiting for. Go on ahead, I'll join you in a moment.

(FLAEMMCHEN exits.
As PREYSING takes the radiogram and reads it, BELLMAN waits for tip, but PREYSING, too engrossed, hands him envelope instead. BELLMAN exits grumpily.)

DOCTOR. *(Behind him.)* "Sorry to report the Boston merger is off."

(MUSIC CUE #7: THE CROOKED PATH)

PREYSING. (*Turns away, his hopes dashed.*) Damn! Damn! Bankruptcy! (*When HE turns Downstage again, his manner is altered.*)
ONCE UPON A TIME A LAD
OUT UPON A STROLL,
CAME UPON AN OLD CROW
PERCHED UPON A POLE.
THE POLE STOOD AT A CROSSROADS,
WHICH COULD THE RIGHT ROAD BE?
"CAW CAW,"
SAID THE CROW,
AND THEN, WHADDAYA KNOW,
HE BLINKED AND MUTTERED
  MEPHISTOPHICALLY:

"TAKE THE CROOKED PATH, LAD,
WALK THE CROOKED MILE!
SKIP THE STRAIGHT AND NARROW—
IT IS OUT OF STYLE!
TAKE THE CROOKED PATH, BOY,
GIVE YOURSELF A BREAK:
NO ONE EVER MADE A LIVING
GIVING
WHEN HE HAD THE CHANCE TO TAKE!"

(*In the 1989-92 Broadway production, PREYSING sang the above well Downstage. Then, at this point, the stage behind him was lighted and revealed to be full of LOBBY DENIZENS ... HE walked backward and CAST surrounded him and sang "CAW CAW!"*)

COMPANY.
"CAW CAW!"
PREYSING.
"TAKE!"
COMPANY.
"CAW CAW!"

PREYSING.
"TAKE THE CROOKED PATH, LAD,
WALK THE CROOKED MILE!
ON THE STRAIGHT AND NARROW
PEOPLE SELDOM SMILE!

ON THE BENDING LANE, LAD,
YOU CAN LIVE CONTENT!
TAKE THE STRAIGHT AND NARROW
AND YOU WILL FOREVER WONDER
WHERE THE BENT—ONE—WENT!"

DID HE? DIDN'T HE?
SHOULD I? SHOULDN'T I?
COULD IT BE INTEGRITY'S A FLAW?
I DON'T KNOW, OLD CROW,
WHERE TO GO, OLD CROW!
CAW! CAW! CAW!

*(HE crumples and after a moment exits, as SCULLERY
    WORKERS enter from opposite side of the stage.)*

    SCULLERY WORKERS. *(Crossing.)*
THEY'RE IN HERE SPENDING MONEY,
A MILLION MARKS A DAY!
WE'RE ONE STEP FROM THE STREET
MAKING JUST ENOUGH TO EAT
FOR A DAY, WEEK, MONTH, YEAR!
SOME HAVE, SOME HAVE NOT!
    GUNTHER GUSTAFSSON.
WHY?

SCENE 6

The Baron's bedroom.
*The CHAUFFEUR lolls on a chaise longue, idly cleaning
    his gun. The BARON enters; HE's dressing.*

BARON. Need I remind you that this is my room? Take your feet off the furniture.

CHAUFFEUR. My boss wants payment now, Baron. You swank around the most expensive hotel in Europe, sign for drinks, food, flowers—

BARON. I have a talent for living.

CHAUFFEUR. What you need is a talent for *paying*. You know, Baron, time is running out for your kind. How will you survive when your looks go? Take my advice and find a rich widow.

BARON. I am not a gigolo.

CHAUFFEUR. Oh, bravo. Well, there's another way. You're sort of likable and I don't want to hurt you. We saw a necklace last night God made just for breaking up. Diamonds that big! Rubies even bigger! It's right here in the hotel, Baron, one flight down. You wouldn't even have to take the lift.

BARON. What makes you think I'd ever steal?

CHAUFFEUR. You'd do anything you'd have to, to keep living your sweet life.

BARON. I would never steal!—except as a last resort.

CHAUFFEUR. How's this for a last resort? (*HE jams gun into the Baron's ribs.*) Just have the money by midnight tomorrow. Midnight tomorrow. Or you'll simply disappear. Got that, Baron?

(*HE exits. The BARON, slightly shaken, stares after him for a moment. Then HE shrugs it off.*)

BARON. Something will turn up. (*Smiles and sings.*)
DANGEROUS GAME
AND A CAREFREE EXISTENCE!
ONLY FOR THOSE
WITH THE COURAGE TO PLAY,
AND THE MONEY TO PAY—

BUYING LIFE
AS IT SHOULD BE!

WILL BE!

*(In Broadway production, the BARON walked into
DANCING PEOPLE.)*

SCENE 7

(MUSIC CUE #8: YELLOW PAVILION)

*We see and hear that we're in the hotel's cabaret-dance
room, called the Yellow Pavilion. PEOPLE dance
Upstage; Downstage KRINGELEIN and DOCTOR
cross, not seeing each other, en route to different
destinations.*
*FLAEMMCHEN enters; as SHE hears the music SHE
moves in rhythm. Then a young, uniformed maid in
the hotel, TRUDE, enters and sees her.*
*KRINGELEIN takes a seat Downstage Right and
pantomimes ordering a cocktail from a WAITER or
BARGIRL.*

TRUDE. Frieda? Frieda, hello!
FLAEMMCHEN. My God! Trude! Hello. How's
your mother?
TRUDE. Still whoring for American officers. How's
yours?
FLAEMMCHEN. Who knows?
TRUDE. Well, so it goes. I'm saving up to take the
Graf Zeppelin to America. Chicago, maybe. I want to go
to a speakeasy! (*Miming peephole.*) Joe sent me.
FLAEMMCHEN. It's Hollywood, California for
me. I want to be in the talkies!—all singing, all dancing—
no typing!

TRUDE. Good luck. Where did you get the money?

FLAEMMCHEN. I haven't yet. Trude, I think I may be pregnant.

TRUDE. Well, so it goes. (*SHE exits. Applause segue.*)

(MUSIC CUE #8A: INTRO–WHO COULDN'T
DANCE WITH YOU)

(The BARON strides in and goes directly to his "appointment": FLAEMMCHEN.)

FLAEMMCHEN. You think I came here looking for you, don't you?

BARON. No, of course not. I came looking for you, to be burned alive in Flaemmchen's flaming embrace.

FLAEMMCHEN. (*Laughing.*) Oh, how you talk!

(THEY start to dance onto the dance area, but KRINGELEIN interrupts them.)

KRINGELEIN. Oh, Baron, sir—my friend—if it weren't for you I wouldn't be part of this wonderland, this wonderful wonderland! Look at all these people with nothing to do but make pleasure—! and you should see my room! I've a real goose-down quilt on my bed—! (*Then to Flaemmchen.*)—Pardon me, my name is Kringelein, Otto Kringelein.

FLAEMMCHEN. Flaemmchen.

KRINGELEIN. (*To the Baron.*)—And you've never seen such a bathroom! Would you believe there's a telephone in it? One can telephone while—

BARON. (*Hastily fleeing.*) Excuse us.

(THEY dance onto the dance area.)

KRINGELEIN. (*Calling after them.*) —bathing!

FLAEMMCHEN. (*As THEY dance sexily.*) He called you Baron. Are you really a baron??

BARON. Baron Felix Amadeus Benvenuto von Gaigern ... Flaemmchen, Flaemmchen, you shake a wicked leg!

(MUSIC CUE #8B: WHO COULDN'T DANCE
WITH YOU)

FLAEMMCHEN. (*Sings as THEY dance.*)
WELL, WHO COULDN'T DANCE WITH YOU?
YOU SWEEP A LADY OFF HER FEET, MISTER!
WHO COULDN'T DANCE WITH YOU?
YOU ARE SO BEAUTIFULLY ON THE BEAT,
     MISTER!

THE BAND IS PLAYING,
WE'RE ON THE FLOOR,
THE MUSIC'S THERE TO BE SHARED.
I USED TO BE FRIGHTENED BEFORE
BUT HERE IN YOUR ARMS I'M NOT SCARED!

WHO WOULDN'T WALTZ THROUGH SPACE?
YOU KEEP A LADY ON HER TOES, MISTER!
MY STEPS ARE COMMONPLACE
BUT YOU MAKE POETRY OUT OF PROSE,
     MISTER!

SO LET THERE BE RHYTHM
AND LET IT BE LOUD!
THE TUNE CAN BE SMOOTH
OR BOUNCY OR BLUE;
I'LL MAKE YOU PROUD!
JUST WATCH ME DANCE!
WHO COULDN'T DANCE WITH YOU?

BARON. (*Dancing her toward Kringlein.*) I want to ask you a little favor.

FLAEMMCHEN. Yes, Baron, whatever it is.

BARON. Dance with Mister Kringelein over there? He's some kind of innocent provincial. Made his pile— now all of a sudden wants to enjoy life—and doesn't know how. I'm afraid he's rather ill.

FLAEMMCHEN. That's too bad, poor man.

BARON. Look at his shirt collar. It's two inches too big for him. He seems to be wasting away.

FLAEMMCHEN. Well, of course I'll dance with him.

(THEY cross to Kringelein.)

FLAEMMCHEN. Mister Kringelein—

KRINGELEIN. Hello, could I offer you two beautiful people a cocktail? The barman just recommended something called a Louisiana Flip. I wonder, is it kosher?

BARON. I'm afraid I can't, Old Socks, the New York Stock Exchange will be opening in minutes. Are you interested in the stock market, Mister Kringelein?

KRINGELEIN. Oh no, I never gamble.

BARON. Pity.

KRINGELEIN. Pity?

BARON. That's how these people can afford to spend their days "making pleasure," as you put it.

KRINGELEIN. *(Lights going on.)* Oh! So that's how they do it. Stocks! I see!

FLAEMMCHEN. Mister Kringelein—

KRINGELEIN. No, Otto.

FLAEMMCHEN.—Otto, could I please have the next dance?

KRINGELEIN. With me?

FLAEMMCHEN. Yes, with you.

K R I N G E L E I N . With me! My God! *(KRINGELEIN stands up—and his pants droop severely; HE has to stop to hitch them up.)*

BARON. Your trousers.

KRINGELEIN. Oh, excuse me—I've been reducing lately.

BARON. Should I introduce you to my tailor?

KRINGELEIN. Would you, please.

BARON. And if you like, the stock ticker. (*To Flaemmchen.*) The American Bar. Five o'clock tomorrow.

FLAEMMCHEN. Oh, yes. (*To Kringelein as the Baron goes.*) Let's go shake a wicked leg!

KRINGELEIN. I've never danced before. Since my uncle died, I'm the only Jew in Fredersdorf. Who'd dance with me?

(*THEY dance; KRINGELEIN is helpless at first, then slowly begins getting the hang of it.*)

FLAEMMCHEN.
WELL, WHO COULDN'T DANCE WITH YOU?
YOU SWEEP A LADY OFF HER FEET, MISTER!
WHO COULDN'T DANCE WITH YOU?
YOU ARE SO BEAUTIFULLY ON THE BEAT—

(*Spoken.*) You're doing very, very well—

KRINGELEIN. I hope I don't step on your feet, Miss Flaemmchen.

FLAEMMCHEN. Don't worry, Otto—you're light as a feather.

KRINGELEIN. I am? Oh, yes. I suppose I am. (*As HE gains confidence, HE sings.*)
WELL, WHO COULDN'T DANCE WITH YOU?
YOU SWEEP A PERSON OFF HIS FEET, LADY!
WHO COULDN'T DANCE WITH YOU?
YOU ARE SO BEAUTIFULLY ON THE BEAT, LADY!
THE BAND IS PLAYING,
WE'RE ON THE FLOOR,
THE MUSIC'S THERE TO BE SHARED.
I USED TO BE NERVOUS BEFORE

BUT HERE IN YOUR ARMS, I'M NOT SCARED!

WHO WOULDN'T WALTZ THROUGH SPACE?
   FLAEMMCHEN.
WE'LL DANCE TO JUPITER AND MARS!
   KRINGELEIN.
YOU MAKE A MAN FEEL TEN FEET TALL, LADY!
I MAY BE SHORT ON GRACE,
   FLAEMMCHEN.
WE'LL PUT OUR FOOTPRINTS ON THE STARS!
   KRINGELEIN.
BUT MY HEART IS ANYTHING BUT SMALL,
   LADY!
   KRINGELEIN and FLAEMMCHEN.
SO LET THERE BE RHYTHM
AND LET IT BE LOUD!
   KRINGELEIN.
I'VE DREAMED ABOUT THIS SINCE I WAS JUST
   TWO!
   FLAEMMCHEN.
AND I HAVE TOO!
   KRINGELEIN.
I'LL MAKE YOU PROUD!
   FLAEMMCHEN.
MY HEART WILL FLY!
   KRINGELEIN.
I KNOW I'LL DANCE!
   FLAEMMCHEN.
AND SO WILL I!
   KRINGELEIN and FLAEMMCHEN.
WHO COULDN'T DANCE ...

(PREYSING approaches them impatiently, and interrupts.)

   PREYSING. Miss Flaemmchen ...
   FLAEMMCHEN. Oh, half a mo, Mister Preysing—

KRINGELEIN. Good evening, Mister Managing Director Preysing.

PREYSING. Have we met?

KRINGELEIN. Met? Met? I'm the bookkeeper who saved you a hundred thousand marks in that Estonian error—Kringelein, Otto!

(KRINGELEIN holds out his hand, but PREYSING ignores it.)

PREYSING. I'm busy, Mister Otto. Flaemmchen—

KRINGELEIN. Yes, well, we're extremely busy too! Busy dancing! The young lady will be with you as soon as we are quite entirely finished with our fox trot!

PREYSING. Miss, I will wait for you in the conference room.

FLAEMMCHEN. Yes, sir.

(PREYSING starts Off; KRINGELEIN follows, pushing through the Dancing People.)

KRINGELEIN. I'm also the bookkeeper who analyzed that Bavarian Company statement! How much did *that* save you?

PREYSING. I'll wait exactly five minutes, Miss Flaemmchen—*(HE starts Off.)*

KRINGELEIN. *(Following, and screaming at him.)* I'll tell you how much that saved you—it saved you millions! *Millions of marks!* And I thank you for the raise I didn't get—and for remembering my name, I don't think!

(But PREYSING is gone. KRINGELEIN comes back Down to Flaemmchen.)

KRINGELEIN. I shouldn't have done that.

FLAEMMCHEN. Will you lose your job?

KRINGELEIN. No, I already quit. It's your job I'm worried about.

FLAEMMCHEN. Oh, don't worry about that!

KRINGELEIN. Why not?

FLAEMMCHEN. What do I need with a job? I'm practically a baroness!

KRINGELEIN. Oh, I see!

FLAEMMCHEN. Let's fox trot!

(THEY dance; SHE coaxes him back to good humor. As THEY disappear amid the DANCING PEOPLE, DOCTOR crosses Downstage.)

DOCTOR. Look at him—dancing! Dancing as if his body were sound, as if his life would go on forever! How we cling to all this nonsense!

(MUSIC CUE #9: MUSIC IS ON)

SCENE 8

A Meeting Room in the hotel.
MANY SHAREHOLDERS are present, facing PREYSING. MANY are smoking cigarettes or cigars. ZINNOWITZ hovers near him as secretary of the company. FLAEMMCHEN hands out statements to ALL THE SHAREHOLDERS.

SHAREHOLDERS.
WHAT'S THE NEWS FROM MASSACHUSETTS?
ANY CABLEGRAM TODAY?
WHAT'S THE NEWS FROM MASSACHUSETTS?
ANY CABLEGRAM TODAY?

FIRST STOCKHOLDER. If you don't have Boston, are there any other American companies showing interest?

PREYSING. I did not say we don't have Boston! A merger is not important to us! What should matter to you shareholders is our past record of profits—profits which will come again! Of course they'll come again!

SHAREHOLDERS. When ...?? Yes, when, Preysing ...? Boston merger or liquidate, I say ...! Let's vote ...! Yes, vote! Vote! Vote! [etc.]

2ND SHAREHOLDER. Point of order. Read the motion before us!

SHAREHOLDERS. Read the motion!

PREYSING. Mister Zinnowitz, read the damn thing.

ZINNOWITZ. The motion is—(*Reads from notes.*) "In the absence of a firm offer from Boston, and in view of the heavy operating losses incurred, the employment of the General Director Preysing is terminated."

(SHAREHOLDERS: Moans and jeers, etc.)

PREYSING. Terminated—

ZINNOWITZ. (*Sings to Preysing.*)

ZINNOWITZ	COMPANY.
	WHAT'S THE NEWS FROM MASSACHUSETTS?
	IS THE BOSTON MERGER ON?
TAKE THE CROOKED PATH, BOY,	WHAT'S THE NEWS FROM MASSACHUSETTS?
GIVE YOURSELF A BREAK.	
NO ONE EVER MADE A LIVING	IS THE BOSTON MERGER ON?
GIVING	WHAT'S THE NEWS FROM MASSACHUSETTS?
WHEN HE HAD THE CHANCE TO TAKE!	IS THE BOSTON MERGER ON?

WHAT'S THE NEWS
FROM
MASSACHUSETTS?
WHAT'S THE NEWS
FROM
MASSACHUSETTS?
TAKE THE CROOKED   IS THE BOSTON
 PATH, BOY,   MERGER ON?
WALK THE CROOKED
 MILE.
TAKE THE CROOKED   (REPEAT)
 PATH—
ON THE STRAIGHT   WHAT'S THE NEWS
 AND NARROW   FROM
                    MASSACHUSETTS?
PEOPLE SELDOM   IS THE BOSTON
 SMILE!   MERGER ON?

DOCTOR. Take the crooked path, boy ... CAW! CAW! CAW!

(PREYSING steps up among the Shareholders, takes from his pocket the radiogram he received earlier, and waves it in the air.)

PREYSING. Ladies and gentlemen—I have just received a radiogram—from America—The Boston merger is definitely—on!
SHAREHOLDERS.
THE BOSTON MERGER!
THE BOSTON MERGER!

(A SHAREHOLDER reaches for the radiogram in Preysing's hand but PREYSING quickly pockets it and steps aside.)

PREYSING. *(To himself, exultantly.)* My God—I did it! I did it!

(SEVERAL STOCKHOLDERS lift PREYSING and carry him out in triumph.)

PREYSING.	**SHAREHOLDERS.**
CAW!	THE BOSTON MERGER!
CAW!	THE BOSTON MERGER!
CAW!	THE BOSTON MERGER!
CAW!	THE BOSTON MERGER!
	IS *ON!*

SCENE 9

Far Upstage we see what seems to be the stage of the theater where Grushinskaya is dancing. GRUSHINSKAYA. is facing her audience Off Up.

As GRUSHINSKAYA, back to us, dances part of her "Giselle," we hear:

COMPANY.
"FIRE AND ICE,
PASSION AND SHEER PERFECTION.
ON THE STAGE
FEARLESSLY FLYING!"
FIRE AND ICE!
FIRE AND ICE!
FIRE AND ICE!
FIRE AND ICE!

SCENE 10

The Financial Corner of the lobby.

The BARON and KRINGELEIN approach a period stock ticker. The BARON picks up a long tape, finds a quote, hands it to KRINGELEIN.

BARON. Here! Look! Radio Corporation of America—hot, hot stock! Hot! If one had bought a couple of hundred shares last week—well, one would be able to afford *many* new suits! And evening clothes?

KRINGELEIN. Baron, what do I need with evening clothes? Except to be buried in.

BARON. It's crazy not to own stocks today. A famous American broker is in the hotel right now. Why not meet him? Why not take a little flyer in the market, Old Socks? (*Starts to lead KRINGELEIN Off.*)

KRINGELEIN. My God, "Old Socks," me buy stocks? Me? Now that would be a *meshugana* thing to do!

(KRINGELEIN exits. CHAUFFEUR enters and holds the BARON back for a moment to confide.)

CHAUFFEUR. That necklace belongs to the ballerina in room 510. This is her big opening night—get it while she's busy at the theater.

SCENE 11

(MUSIC CUE #9A: GRU'S BEDROOM)

Backstage at Ballet Theater, and the facade or roof of Grand Hotel.

(GRUSHINSKAYA is finishing GISELLE. SHE drops to the floor in a low, grand bow. From her audience comes a sibilant hiss, a few chuckles, a scatter of insultingly light applause. GRUSHINSKAYA bolts and runs off the ballet stage and into Raffaela's arms.)

(BARON appears elsewhere onstage, climbing up portal or edge of set ...)

GRUSHINSKAYA.
Did you hear? Did you hear? Oh, my God, they hated me!

RAFFAELA.
No, no, Madame, they loved you.

(BARON makes his way along a grid or ladder at considerable risk to life and limb.)

GRUSHINSKAYA.
Loved? No applause! *No encore!*

RAFFAELA.
Madame, you must change for the swan—

GRUSHINSKAYA.
(Hands Raffaela some article of costuming.) Get understudy ready. I am never going back on a stage. *(Starts off; RAFFAELA holds her back.)*

(BARON reaches what seems to be Grushinskaya's terrace.)

RAFFAELA.
Madame, no!—Where are you going?
GRUSHINSKAYA.
Go back to hotel! No encore! No encore! (*Runs off sobbing.*)

(*RAFFAELA, torn, starts to follow, but then hurries in opposite direction, calling.*)

RAFFAELA.
Get Madame's understudy ready! Madame is ill!

(*GRUSHINSKAYA is seen running frantically, perhaps pushing passerbys aside.*)

GRUSHINSKAYA.
No encore! No encore! :
COMPANY.
"FIRE AND ICE!
FIRE AND ICE!
FIRE AND ICE!
FIRE AND ICE!"
GRUSHINSKAYA. No encore!
COMPANY.
"NO ENCORE!"

(*BARON gets into her room.*)

(*BARON finds a handful of her clothes—holds them up admiringly—goes on rummaging, but not finding necklace ...*)

SCENE 12

GRUSHINSKAYA's Suite.

The BARON finds necklace—admires it. HE starts to exit through window just as GRUSHINSKAYA arrives at door ... HE hears her—hastily retreats—hides as SHE enters, sobbing. SHE takes off some of her ballet costume—flings things to the floor. SHE discovers the BARON—cries out.

BARON. Please don't be frightened!

GRUSHINSKAYA. What—what the hell're you doing here? *(Backing away.)* I've seen you—what're you doing here? *(Grabs telephone; into telephone.)* Hello—

(Gently but firmly HE takes telephone from her and puts it back in its cradle.)

BARON. I will tell you the truth, madame—I have come here—*(Searching.)*—to breathe the air you breathe.

GRUSHINSKAYA. "To breathe the air I breathe?" *(SHE picks up telephone again.)* I am calling management!

BARON. *(Hastily.)* No!—You see, it is not the first time I have done this. Many a night in many a city I have come to your rooms while you were at the theatre. I am a fan, Madame, an abject fan ... An abject fan ... who loves you.

GRUSHINSKAYA. *(SHE regards him.)* Better. *(SHE hangs up the telephone.)* You have come too late, young man. Whatever it was you loved has deserted me. Grushinskaya is finished. Grushinskaya has danced for the last time.

BARON. You can't mean that! What happens when I see you dance is what happens when I hear great music.

GRUSHINSKAYA. *Quel compliment!* You are musician? You know music?

BARON. I am German. Of the same blood as Beethoven and Brahms.

GRUSHINSKAYA. I have seen you. You are a guest here?

BARON. Yes. I live just upstairs. (*The BARON produces—and flashes—his expensive cigarette case; HE begins to light a cigarette.*)

GRUSHINSKAYA. No cigarettes, please. Smoke is bad for me. (*Holds his hand and examines cigarette case.*) Such riches!

BARON. Thank you. (*HE lights his cigarette.*) You're a dancer, not a singer.

GRUSHINSKAYA. Some women find insolence attractive. I am not one of them. Go now, leave me.

BARON. Forgive me, madame. Sometimes I do dumb things. (*HE puts out the cigarette.*)

GRUSHINSKAYA. When did you see me dance?

BARON. Monte Carlo. You danced *Romeo and Juliet.*

GRUSHINSKAYA. My God! That was my *first* farewell tour. How old are you? If you don't mind my asking.

BARON. The truth? I am twenty-nine years—(*A beat.*)—and twenty-nine months. And you, Madame?

GRUSHINSKAYA. And me what? My age? Are you crazy?

BARON. "If you don't mind my asking."

GRUSHINSKAYA. (*Pause, then smiling.*) Why not? I am forty-nine years—(*A beat.*)—and forty-nine months.

(*THEY laugh.*)

GRUSHINSKAYA. So. Now our moment has concluded. Go.

BARON. On the contrary, our moment has not yet begun.

(MUSIC CUE #10: LOVE CAN'T HAPPEN)

GRUSHINSKAYA. (*Sings to herself.*)
WHAT IS THIS? WHO CAN THIS BE?

MY GOD! BUT THIS IS CHARMING!
SUDDENLY A YOUNG AND HANDSOME
  STRANGER IN MY ROOM ...
WHY IS IT, IN SPITE OF THAT, HE DOESN'T SEEM
ALARMING? BUT
CHARMING! CHARMING.
(To him.)
  Where else have you seen me dance?

BARON. *(Sings.)*
MADEMOISELLE, I HAVE FOLLOWED YOU
  EVERYWHERE,
ALMOST THROUGHOUT YOUR CAREER:
LONDON, VIENNA, PARIS, (PAR-EE)
I'VE ADMIRED YOU,
HOPING ONE DAY
WE MIGHT MEET IN THIS WAY,
THOUGH I NEVER THOUGHT I'D BE CARRIED
  AWAY.
OH, I KNEW YOU'D BE BEAUTIFUL,
BUT NOT SO BEAUTIFUL ...!
(To himself.)
WHY AM I TALKING THIS WAY?
CAN THIS BE REAL TO ME?
NONSENSE, MY BOY,
YOU KNEW SHE WAS BEAUTIFUL,
BUT NOT SO BEAUTIFUL ...!
(To her.)
LOVE CAN'T HAPPEN QUITE SO QUICKLY,
NOT UNLESS I DREAMED YOU
BEAUTIFULLY AND SWEETLY ...

NO, DON'T LOOK THROUGH ME SO CLEARLY,
I MIGHT VERY NEARLY LOSE MYSELF
COMPLETELY!
WHO COULD EVER HAVE SUSPECTED
YOU WOULD MAKE ME TREMBLE SO?

I CAN'T THINK OF ANY ANSWER
OTHER THAN, IF LOVE COMES ...
WHEN LOVE COMES,
YOU KNOW!
(*To himself.*)
WHAT IS THIS I'M SAYING?
WHAT IS THIS I'M FEELING?
LIKE I'M GETTING DRUNK LOOKING IN HER
   EYES!
OVERWHELMING FACE—UTTERLY
   APPEALING—
NEVER MIND THE TRUTH, NEVER MIND THE
   LIES,
NEVER MIND A THOUGHT IN THE WORLD
   EXCEPT

LOVE CAN'T HAPPEN QUITE SO QUICKLY,
BUT I'M FILLED WITH NO ONE BUT HER!
   GRUSHINSKAYA. Please, why are you *really*
here?
   BARON. I told you.
   GRUSHINSKAYA. I don't believe you. You are
so young. I have toe shoes older than you.
   BARON. (*Laughing.*) Does that matter?
   GRUSHINSKAYA. I am not so young.
   BARON. Did you think I thought you were? I told
you you're very beautiful.
   GRUSHINSKAYA. For my age.
   BARON. Age has nothing to do with beauty. Some
women grow more beautiful as they grow older.
   GRUSHINSKAYA. There is too much light—turn
it off—
   BARON. (*Stopping her.*) No! I want to see you.
   GRUSHINSKAYA. See what? My lines—?
   BARON. Your *life.* It's all there on your face. Your
remarkable life. Your courage, your strength, your
sacrifice, your experience. I'm tired of empty,
inexperienced faces—

(THEY sing.)

GRUSHINSKAYA.
LEAVE ON THE LIGHT,
IT'S BEEN SO LONG!

LOVE CAN'T HAPPEN
  QUITE SO
  QUICKLY—
BUT WHAT CAN THIS
  BE THEN TO ME?　　　　**BARON.**
　　　　　　　　　　NOT A THOUGHT IN
　　　　　　　　　　　THE WORLD EXCEPT
　　　　　　　　　　　YOU!

NO, DON'T HOLD ME
  QUITE SO CLOSELY:
IF YOU HOLD ME
  CLOSELY
I MIGHT BREAK!
  BARON.
NO, DON'T LOOK THROUGH ME SO CLEARLY,
I MIGHT VERY NEARLY LOSE MYSELF
COMPLETELY!

WHO COULD EVER HAVE SUSPECTED
I WOULD BE HERE TREMBLING SO?
I CAN'T THINK OF ANY ANSWER
OTHER THAN, IF LOVE COMES ...
WHEN LOVE COMES,
YOU KNOW ...

AND I KNOW!

SCENE 13

(MUSIC CUE #11: WHAT YOU NEED)

The DOCTOR is seen in a pinpoint of light.

DOCTOR. Even in Grand Hotel the lights finally go out—except in chambers of discontent—

(LIGHTS come up on an indication of Raffaela's small room.
RAFFAELA is putting ribbons on a pair of Grushinskaya's ballet slippers.)

RAFFAELA. *(Speaking to slippers.)* Oh, Elizaveta, Elizaveta, dearest—*(Sings.)*
WHAT YOU NEED IS SOMEONE STRONG
TO LEAN UPON WHEN YOU'RE LOW.

WHAT YOU NEED
IS SOMEONE WISE TO COUNT UPON AS YOU GO.

WHAT I AM
IS FAR FROM STRONG,
AND FAR FROM WISE,
OH FAR INDEED!

YET SUDDENLY,
WHEN YOU'RE NEAR TO ME,
I FEEL SOMEHOW STRONG,
IN SOME WAY WISE,
LIKE SOMEONE WHO'S
WHAT YOU NEED!

SCENE 14

An indication of a portion of a hotel conference room is on one side of stage, and a portion of lobby or corridor is indicated on the other side.
In the conference room, PREYSING stands behind FLAEMMCHEN who is seated, typing or working on some papers. HE seems to be inhaling her scent.

PREYSING. Flaemmchen—That's a provocative scent you're wearing. Do men give you expensive presents?

FLAEMMCHEN. No! I bought it myself. I get a discount. Do you want some for your wife? I could get you a discount too.

PREYSING. That won't be necessary. Flaemmchen, I must go to Boston, in America. One must take charge of one's life! Make things happen!

FLAEMMCHEN. Yes, sir?

PREYSING. I'll need a secretary. To take care of me. I, uh, wondered—

FLAEMMCHEN. (*Hastily, turning away.*) I better finish your letters.

(LIGHTS come up on the other side of stage as they go down on FLAEMMCHEN and PREYSING. ERIK enters what might be a corridor or other backstairs area carrying a dustpan on a pole. ROHNA enters behind him.)

ROHNA. (*Sharply.*) Litnauer!

ERIK. Sir!

ROHNA. Apparently you don't like working here.

ERIK. Sir, I like it a lot.

ROHNA. (*HE touches Erik's cheek.*) Stubble. Most untidy.

ERIK. I was at hospital! My wife may be dying! Dying!

ROHNA. Wife! I have a wife too. A wife who's ill. Do you hear me mewling around about it?

ERIK. No, sir, I didn't even know you were married.

ROHNA. Damn your wife! Get to work!

(ERIK exits; ROHNA follows him Off as LIGHTS come up on PREYSING and FLAEMMCHEN.)

FLAEMMCHEN. *(Hands letters to Preysing.)* Are they all right, sir?

PREYSING. *(Scans paper.)* You're a very good secretary. Now—about going to Boston.—Did I make myself clear? I want someone who'd—be nice to me. Understand?

FLAEMMCHEN. Yes, I understand. Is Boston near Hollywood?

PREYSING. Only a train ride away.

(HE exits. SHE watches him go. LIGHTS down on FLAEMMCHEN and up on ERIK who is shovelling some dust into his dustpan. ROHNA enters to him. HE touches Erik's face again.)

ROHNA. I meant to say, I have a razor in my room you could use.

ERIK. There's one in the staff dressing room. *(Pulls away.)*

ROHNA. *(Offended.)* I see. I thought I saw a certain fineness in you ... *(HE drops burning cigarette to floor.)* Apparently I was wrong. Litnauer, I fear for your future here. *(Exits.)*

(Cowed and frightened, ERIK picks up the cigarette butt in dustpan and faces Down, deeply worried ... LIGHTS come up to include FLAEMMCHEN who now also faces Down, also deeply worried.)

SCENE 15

Raffaela's room. Perhaps SHE is closing suitcase.

RAFFAELA. (*Spoken.*) Oh, Elizaveta, dear—
(*Sings.*)
SUDDENLY
WHEN YOU'RE NEAR TO ME,
I FEEL SOMEHOW STRONG,
IN SOME WAY WISE,
LIKE SOMEONE WHO'S
WHAT YOU NEED!

(LIGHT dims on RAFFAELA; spot comes up on the DOCTOR.)

DOCTOR. Sometimes the touch of strangers triggers a passion that penetrates to the spine. But in the morning? Lovers—or strangers again?

SCENE 16

Grushinskaya's Suite again.
There's a sense of morning in the lighting. GRUSHINSKAYA is asleep. The BARON enters, finishing dressing. Some of his clothes are on the floor. HE finds necklace in his pocket ... goes to table where HE found it and is just returning it to its place when GRUSHINSKAYA sits up in bed.

GRUSHINSKAYA. *Qu'est-ce que tu fais?* What are you doing?
BARON. Uh—admiring your necklace. Beautiful! I enjoy beautiful jewelry.
GRUSHINSKAYA. So I notice.

BARON. What? Did you think I was stealing it?

GRUSHINSKAYA. If you want it, take it, take it, whoever you are!

BARON. (*Returns necklace to its box and snaps it shut.*) I am Baron Felix Amadeus Benvenuto von Gaigern.

GRUSHINSKAYA. A baron! Then you must *really* need money.

BARON. (*HE crosses to her.*) Elizaveta—your beautiful name! Elizaveta, what's the matter? We were so happy last night. I was.

GRUSHINSKAYA. But now it's morning. You have put clothes on. Of course now you want to go.

BARON. I want to stay here and make love to you again. And again after that.

GRUSHINSKAYA. My God! No one is *that* young. Are you really a baron?

BARON. It's a very small title.

GRUSHINSKAYA. I have always attracted aristocrats. They are not reliable. They are too successful with women. You must have known a great many.

BARON. I've known a few girls. I've never known a woman until last night. I've never known such a combination of passion and tenderness. Elizaveta—Elizaveta—I have to confess something—something you won't like—

GRUSHINSKAYA. I knew it! You're married!

BARON. Oh, no—worse than that. I came here to steal your necklace.

GRUSHINSKAYA. So. So. Well—why tell me now?

BARON. Because if I didn't, you'd never believe me when I say "I love you."

GRUSHINSKAYA. Say you love me—*now*. With your clothes on.

BARON. I love you—I love you!

(MUSIC CUE #11A: BEFORE BONJOUR AMOUR)

GRUSHINSKAYA. I want to believe it—I do believe it! Yes! (*Kisses him.*) And now I must confess to you. I want to dance! I've been lying here thinking. You make me young again! Yesterday I cancelled Vienna, but I'm going to go! And you're going with me! Yes, Baron von Gaigern???
BARON. To Vienna? When?
GRUSHINSKAYA. Tomorrow morning. You will come! Yes?
BARON. Leaving town right now would be— extremely difficult.
GRUSHINSKAYA. I see. Business?
BARON. I haven't any money.
GRUSHINSKAYA. I'll give you money.
BARON. Elizaveta! I am not a gigolo!
GRUSHINSKAYA. Of course not. I'm sorry. Come to Vienna, *please*—I need you. I am half dead without you! I need you.
BARON. (*Figuring.*) Vienna. Well, why not? I'll find a way. I always manage somehow. Of course I'll come with you! I'll meet you at the railway station—with my arms full of roses! *Red* roses for passion. Elizaveta, it's our first morning!—Bonjour!

(HE exits. SHE is ecstatic.)

(MUSIC CUE #12: BONJOUR AMOUR)

GRUSHINSKAYA. Bonjour! (*SHE sings.*)
BONJOUR, AMOUR?
HELLO TO LOVE,
HELLO, MY LIFE!
BONJOUR!

BONJOUR, AMOUR,
YOU SAVED ME IN THE NICK OF TIME,
BONJOUR!

I NEVER THOUGHT IT WAS POSSIBLE
FOR SOMEONE LIKE THIS TO LOVE ME!
BUT SUDDENLY NOW IT IS POSSIBLE
AND YOU SEE ...

AMOUR! BONJOUR!
AGAIN I LOVE!
HE LOVES!
IT'S LOVE!
BONJOUR!

AMOUR, BONJOUR,
JE L'AIME, IL M'AIME,
ET MOI, JE DIS
BONJOUR!

I KNOW HE'S YOUNG,
SO MANY THINGS ABOUT HIM ARE UNSURE
BUT, TO BE SURE,
I KNOW MY HEART
AND IN MY HEART I SING:

BONJOUR! A L'AMOUR!
THIS BOY! THIS MAN!
HE MAKES ME FEEL A GIRL AGAIN,
BONJOUR!
MY JOY! MY FAN!
HE PUTS ME IN A WHIRL AGAIN,
BONJOUR!

ALREADY I THINK I AM MISSING HIM,
AND I ONLY MET HIM LAST NIGHT.
BUT HOW WONDERFUL TO BE MISSING HIM!
OH, MY LOVE ... OH, MY LIGHT ...

AMOUR! AMOUR!
I CAN'T BELIEVE YOU CAME TO ME,

BONJOUR!
AMOUR! AMOUR!
NOW NOTHING IS THE SAME TO ME,
BONJOUR!

IT'S TRUE, PERHAPS,
IT ALL MAY BE A LITTLE PREMATURE
BUT I AM SURE!
I KNOW MY HEART

AND IN MY HEART I FEEL
THERE IS A MIRACLE OF LOVING
AND A MIRACLE OF LIVING!
AND I CRY WITH ALL MY SOUL TO THIS AMOUR:

BONJOUR!

SCENE 17

(MUSIC CUE #14: THE GRAND CHARLESTON)

The Hotel Bar.
PEOPLE are drinking and dancing the Charleston.

COMPANY.
H-A-P-P-Y
WHY, WHY AM I SO HAPPY
WHEN THEY PLAY THE CHARLESTON?
THE JIMMYS.
D-A-N-D-Y
WHY, WHY DO I FEEL DANDY
WHEN I DANCE THE CHARLESTON?
COME DO THE NEW BEAT
SWEEPING THROUGH THE OLD WORLD,
    WARMING UP A COLD WORLD
HARLEM TO CHINA!

WHAT BEGAN IN CHARLESTON
IS NOW DONE IN LONDON,
EV'RYWHERE FROM PODUNK TO PARIS TO
   PITTSBURGH
TO PEKING TO CHARLESTON IN SOUTH
   CAROLINA!

(FLAEMMCHEN enters and dances happily. Then SHE is joined by the BARON who dances with her. As THEY dance.)

FLAEMMCHEN. When you weren't here at five, I thought, "He's let me down."
BARON. Out of the question. I've been thinking about you all day.
FLAEMMCHEN. Is that the truth? Really?
BARON. Oh, Flaemmchen, I feel like doing something totally mad! I want to bite you or play the fool with you, or pull you about!—(*HE does so.*)
FLAEMMCHEN. You're quite different than you were yesterday.
BARON. Something has happened to me since yesterday to make me different. I fell in love.
FLAEMMCHEN. (*Misunderstanding; delighted.*) Really?
BARON. Yes! Isn't that extraordinary! To find that all of a sudden there's only one woman in the world who excites you—the way she looks, that dear face—oh, she's not nearly as young as you—

(FLAEMMCHEN reacts—tries to pull away from him, but HE goes on rhapsodizing.)

BARON. (*Pointing to Flaemmchen's face.*) She has little wrinkles here—and here—I find her so—she makes me laugh and cry at the same time. She is so utterly delightful that I can't resist her. The simple, absurd fact is: I have found true love.

FLAEMMCHEN. True love? Is there such a thing?

BARON. Yes, yes, there is such a thing, dear Flaemmchen, pretty Flaemmchen.

FLAEMMCHEN. I don't feel very pretty right now.

BARON. Not pretty? Beautiful! How about a Charleston?

FLAEMMCHEN. Consolation prize? Well, sure, why not?

(THEY start to dance as KRINGELEIN enters, wearing an overcoat.)

KRINGELEIN. Baron! Baron! My friend, I know you meant well—but it was you who encouraged me to buy all that radio stock—

BARON. Uh-oh. Sorry. How many points down?

KRINGELEIN. Sixteen!

BARON. I'm so sorry!

KRINGELEIN. Sixteen points—but up! (*HE removes his overcoat, revealing a well-cut dinner jacket.*) Sixteen points up overnight! (*Waves his bulging wallet.*) I made more last night than I ever made in an entire year! And I have you to thank! (*HE kisses the Baron.*) All this money and all I did was *sleep*!

FLAEMMCHEN.	**BARON.**
(Kissing Kringelein.) Oh I'm so glad!	Congratulations, Old Socks!

(ALL THREE laugh and embrace. Then PREYSING appears and beckons to Flaemmchen.)

PREYSING. Flaemmchen—

FLAEMMCHEN. I better not lose this job—All there is, is what there is. Right, Baron? (*SHE exits with PREYSING.*)

KRINGELEIN. Baron, I want to buy drinks for everyone!

BARON. (*Laughing*.) No, Old Socks. No. Put that in a bank.

KRINGELEIN. (*To Barman*.) Oh, sir, please, *two* glasses of champagne for my friend and me. The most highly regarded kind—it's called Mooey something ... I want to drink a toast to my friend here—my distinguished friend who keeps helping me. You will take a glass with me, won't you, Baron?

BARON. Of course I will, Old Socks!

(MUSIC CUE #15: WE'LL TAKE A
GLASS TOGETHER)

THE JIMMYS.
RUB-A-DUB, RUB-A-DUB A-DUB A-DUB,
RUB-A-DUB, RUB-A-DUB A-DUB A-DUB,

KRINGELEIN.	THE JIMMYS.
WE'LL TAKE A GLASS TOGETHER	RUB-A-DUB, RUB-A DUB,
	RUB-A-DUB, RUB-A DUB,
IN CELEBRATION OF OUR MEETING!	RUB-A-DUB, RUB-A DUB,
	RUB-A-DUB, RUB-A DUB,
BARON.	
IN CELEBRATION	RUB-A-DUB, RUB-A DUB,
OR OUR BEING FACE TO FACE:	RUB-A-DUB, RUB-A DUB,

KRINGELEIN.
FRIENDLY,
BARON.
CIVILIZED,
BARON & KRINGELEIN.
MEMBERS OF THE RACE.
BARON.
I'LL DRINK TO YOU.

KRINGELEIN.
NO, I TO YOU.
BARON.
YOU'LL DRINK TO ME.
KRINGELEIN.
THEN YOU TO ME!
BARON.
I'M SURE WE TWO—
KRINGELEIN.
I *KNOW* WE TWO
BARON.
COULD FIND NO FINER COMPANY!
KRINGELEIN.
THANK YOU, BARON!

THE JIMMYS.
RUB-A-DUB, RUB-A
DUB-A-DUB-A-DUB,
RUB-A-DUB, RUB-A
DUB-A-DUB-A-DUB,

BARON.
WE'LL TAKE A GLASS
TOGETHER

RUB-A-DUB, RUB-A-
DUB,
RUB-A-DUB, RUB-A-
DUB,

AND WE WILL LIFT IT

RUB-A-DUB, RUB-A-
DUB,

TO THE GOOD LIFE!

RUB-A-DUB, RUB-A-
DUB,

KRINGELEIN.
AND AS WE'RE
LIFTING IT

THE JIMMYS.

RUB-A-DUB, RUB-A-
DUB,

WE WILL MOST
SINCERELY SAY,

RUB-A-DUB, RUB-A-
DUB,

"PROSIT!"
  BARON.
"YOUR HEALTH, SIR!"
  KRINGELEIN.
"SALUTÉ!"
  BARON.
AND "SKAAL!"
  KRINGELEIN.
"NA ZDROVYE!"
  BARON.
"A VOTRE SANTE!"
  KRINGELEIN and BARON.
FOR ONE WARM MOMENT IN THIS COLD AND
  CARELESS DAY,
WE'LL TAKE A GLASS TOGETHER!
  THE JIMMYS.
RUB-A-DUB, RUB-A-DUB-A-DUB-A-DUB
RUB-A-DUB, RUB-A-DUB
  BARON.
I'LL DRINK TO YOU!
  KRINGELEIN.
NO, *I* TO YOU !
  BARON.
THEN VICE-A VERS!
  KRINGELEIN.
YES, VICE-A VERS!
  BARON.
I'M SURE IT'S TRUE:
  KRINGELEIN.
I *KNOW* IT'S TRUE
  BARON.
THINGS MAY BE BAD BUT COULD BE WORSE!
  KRINGELEIN.
ABSOLUTELY!
  THE JIMMYS.
RUB-A-DUB, RUB-A-DUB, A-DUB-A-DUB
RUB-A-DUB, RUB-A-DUB, A-DUB-A-DUB

BARON.	THE JIMMYS.

BARON.
WE'LL ASK NO WHY
  OR WHETHER,

      RUB-A-DUB, RUB-A-
      DUB,

WE'LL SPEND EACH
  MOMENT,

      RUB-A-DUB, RUB-A-
      DUB,

KRINGELEIN.
YES, WE WILL!
BARON.
AS IT MOVES US.
KRINGELEIN.
AS IT MOVES US.   RUB-A-DUB, RUB-A-
      DUB,

BARON.
COME, COME, MY
  COMRADE,
KRINGELEIN.
COMRADE?   RUB-A-DUB,
BARON & KRINGELEIN.
NIP THE NECTAR OF THE DAY:
KRINGELEIN.
SWEET NECTAR:
BARON.
SHERRY!
KRINGELEIN.
COMPARI!

(During song, KRINGELEIN, out of joy and alcohol, begins to dance, doing a ragged, inexpert and slightly hysterical Charleston in imitation of DANCING PEOPLE who are dancing in the background. Laughing, the BARON helps and joins in.)

BARON.
SCOTCH WHISKEY!

KRINGELEIN.
CHARTREUSE!
BARON.
A COGNAC!
KRINGELEIN and BARON.
AN ABSINTHE FRAPPE!

FOR ONE WARM MOMENT
IN A WORLD GONE COLD AND CRASS,
WE'LL TAKE A GLASS TOGETHER!
COMPANY.
WE'LL TAKE A GLASS TOGETHER
AND WE WILL LIFT IT
TO THE GOOD LIFE!
AND AS WE'RE LIFTING IT
WE WILL MOST SINCERELY SAY,
PROSIT!
YOUR HEALTH, SIR!
SALUTE!
AND SKAAL!
NA ZDROVYE!
A VOTRE SANTE!
FOR ONE WARM MOMENT IN THIS COLD AND
  CARELESS DAY,

*(KRINGELEIN and the BARON dance a wild, and—as
  KRINGELEIN   gets   drunker—out-of-control
  Charleston.)*

GROUP #1.   **GROUP #2.**
WE'LL CELEBRATE!   WE'LL TAKE A GLASS!
WE'LL CELEBRATE!   WE'LL TAKE A GLASS!
WE'LL CELEBRATE!   WE'LL TAKE A GLASS!
WE'LL CELEBRATE!   WE'LL TAKE A GLASS!
WE'LL CELEBRATE!   WE'LL TAKE A GLASS!
WE'LL CELEBRATE!   WE'LL TAKE A GLASS!
WE'LL CELEBRATE!   WE'LL TAKE A GLASS!

ALL.
WE'LL TAKE A GLASS TOGETHER!
WE'LL TAKE A GLASS TOGETHER!
WE'LL TAKE A GLASS TOGETHER!
WE'LL TAKE A GLASS TODAY!

(Exhausted, KRINGELEIN nearly collapses, lurches out of sight for a moment. The BARON, protective, starts to hurry after him, but stops suddenly—sees Kringelein's bulging pocketbook on floor. HE picks it up, starts after Kringelein with wallet in his hand ... walks more and more slowly—stops, stares at the money, the answer to his needs. HE pockets the wallet and starts to hurry Off, skulking a bit, in opposite direction, but KRINGELEIN reappears.)

KRINGELEIN. Oh, Baron—I don't feel so good ...

(HE seems about to collapse. The BARON hesitates, sighs—and hurries back to help Kringelein; and leads him Off, half carrying him.
As THEY exit, FLAEMMCHEN enters, followed by PREYSING, who overtakes her.)

PREYSING. I've been waiting for you in the conference room. Flaemmchen, do I have to find another secretary for my trip?
FLAEMMCHEN. Could I have a thousand marks to start with? Right away? Is that too much?
PREYSING. (*Concealing his relief.*) I might manage it, Flaemmchen.
FLAEMMCHEN. And perhaps something for clothes. I have no clothes. Not what a man like you would consider clothes. You'd want me to look nice, wouldn't you?
PREYSING. We might arrange that. Do you like the idea of going to America?
FLAEMMCHEN. Yes, sir. Very much.

PREYSING. You'd be nice to me?

FLAEMMCHEN. Yes, sir.

PREYSING. Very nice?

FLAEMMCHEN. I'm not a cheat. or a tease.

PREYSING. ... Run home and get your things. I'll book the room connecting to mine.

FLAEMMCHEN. Tonight??

PREYSING. You said you wanted a thousand marks right away. Didn't you mean tonight?

FLAEMMCHEN. Yessir. Yes. Tonight.

(THEY go Off in opposite directions as the CHARLESTON DANCERS and THE JIMMYS take over the stage.)

SCENE 18

The DOCTOR's Room/A Corridor/ FLAEMMCHEN's · Room.

(MUSIC CUE #16: I WALTZ ALONE)

DOCTOR, in pain, is giving himself an injection of morphine. The DANCING COUPLE—and perhaps OTHER COUPLES—waltzes across as the DOCTOR begins to feel better and sings:

DOCTOR.
I'M IN MY ROOM AT NIGHT,
BEHIND A DOOR A GRAMOPHONE
IS FAINTLY, FAINTLY PLAYING,

(Now LIGHTS go up on what seems to be a corridor above stairs ... a BELLBOY, carrying Flaemmchen's small suitcase, is leading PREYSING and FLAEMMCHEN to her room.)

BELLBOY. Has the lady any more luggage?

FLAEMMCHEN. No. The rest of my luggage will come tomorrow.

BELLBOY. Yes, ma'am.

DOCTOR.
AND IN MY ROOM AT NIGHT
I WALTZ ALONE.

BELLBOY. (*Mimes opening a door for them.*) Goodnight, sir. (*Adds slyly.*) And madame.

(*BELLBOY goes Off. PREYSING gestures for FLAEMMCHEN to proceed him into her room. THEY move into darkness, apparently entering the room.*
LIGHTS come up on KRINGELEIN and the BARON on opposite side of stage, KRINGELEIN leaning on the Baron. ERIK follows them ... THEY pause before what we can presume is Kringelein's door. KRINGELEIN, unwell, groans.)

BARON. Open Mister Kringelein's door, please, Erik.

FLAEMMCHEN. Mister Preysing, I'd like to get myself settled—by myself.

DOCTOR.
MY FANCY SOON TAKES FLIGHT:

(*ERIK pantomimes unlocking door. KRINGELEIN and the BARON exit into Kringelein's room. LIGHTS down here and up on an indication of Flaemmchen's bedroom. FLAEMMCHEN and PREYSING are there. HE starts to unbutton her dress.*)

PREYSING. (*Reluctantly.*) As you wish, Flaemmchen. My room connects through here. (*Starts out, but changes his mind.*)

DOCTOR.
I'M IN A PLACE OF PLUSH AND PEARLS,

OF WHIRLING GIRLS, AND COUNTLESS
  CANDLES GLOWING,
    PREYSING. —No. I want to watch you undress.
    FLAEMMCHEN. That's important to you?
    PREYSING. You said you'd be nice to me.
    FLAEMMCHEN. I will—I'm not a cheat. Or a
tease. (*SHE begins to take off her stockings.*)
    DOCTOR.
AS BY MY LAMP'S DIM LIGHT
I WALTZ ALONE.
    PREYSING. —Couldn't you call me something
sweet? Maybe "darling," the way people do in films?
    FLAEMMCHEN. Suppose I got in the habit and
one day I see you and I call out, "Hello, darling"—and
your wife is with you? Or your children. How many do
you have?
    PREYSING. Now you're talking too much. Never
mind stockings, take your dress off.
    FLAEMMCHEN. Sir, I have to go to bathroom.

*(SHE hurries Off into what we can presume is the
bathroom. HE exits irritably into his room. LIGHTS
come up on Kringelein's room. The BARON is
helping KRINGELEIN sink into a chair.)*

    BARON. Feeling better?
    KRINGELEIN. Yes. Let's dance some more.
    BARON. (*Laughing.*) I think you mean it! You've
had enough, Old Socks.
    KRINGELEIN. Why, just because I'm dying?
    BARON. Dying doesn't frighten you? You're a
damned brave fellow!
    KRINGELEIN. It's not dying that frightens me—
it's death.
    BARON. I don't understand the distinction.
    KRINGELEIN. Don't you see? As long as you're
dying, you're still alive. Take my word for it—dying can
take a very long time. The only thing is, you don't want

to die penniless. They won't treat you like a human being. That's why I cashed everything in—so I'd always have it right where I could touch it —(*KRINGELEIN pats his pocket; is surprised to feel nothing; pats another pocket—then another—in growing alarm.*) My pocketbook! Where's my pocketbook! *My pocketbook!*

BARON. You'll make yourself ill again! Forget your damn pocketbook! Lie back!

KRINGELEIN. Forget?? It's everything I own in the world! My savings, my stock winnings, even my burial insurance! I must've dropped it in the bar!—(*HE runs out.*)—where I was dancing around like an idiot!

(The BARON watches him exit. LIGHTS down here.)

DOCTOR.
TWO AND THREE AND ONE TURN— —

(LIGHTS have come up on Flaemmchen's room. PREYSING calls irritably into bathroom.)

PREYSING. Flaemmchen!
FLAEMMCHEN. (*Entering.*) I was fixing my hair. You want me pretty, don't you?
DOCTOR.
THE ROOM GROWS DARK
IT ALMOST SEEMS I'M FLYING!
AM I FLYING?

*(LIGHTS come up on a bit of corridor.
The BARON overtakes KRINGELEIN.)*

BARON. Old Socks! Listen! I absolutely forgot— remember, you gave me your pocketbook to hold? (*HE hands bundle of cash to KRINGELEIN.*)
KRINGELEIN. I did?
BARON. In the bar. You must remember.

(KRINGELEIN stares at the money—takes it very slowly, as HE comprehends what really happened.)

KRINGELEIN. Oh yes. I gave it to you to hold and you said, "If you wish, Old Socks," or something like that ... (*Adds slyly.*) Oh, and I remember something else—yes! I said you had to share in my stock winnings? And you agreed.

BARON. I did?

KRINGELEIN. Yes, you did. (*HE peels off a wad of money and hands it to the BARON.*)

DOCTOR.
TWO AND THREE AND ONE TURN

BARON. (*It's a considerable wad of banknotes.*) But this is—this is terribly generous! Do you mean it, Old Socks?

KRINGELEIN. Please accept it.

DOCTOR.
THAT'S A NEATLY DONE TURN

BARON. Mister Kringelein—Otto—I'll accept this— as a loan. Hold my cigarette case as collateral. (*Hands him the case.*) It's an heirloom. I don't know how it's escaped my creditors—young Erik says it's famous in the hotel.

KRINGELEIN. Collateral—even between friends?

BARON. Especially between friends. I'll come back in a few days and redeem it.

KRINGELEIN. You're going away?

BARON. (*As THEY exit together, waltzing.*) To beautiful Vienna!

COMPANY.
H-A-P-P-Y WHY,
WHY AM I SO HAPPY?

(CHAUFFEUR enters and calls after the Baron.)

CHAUFFEUR. Baron!

(The BARON re-enters alone.)

CHAUFFEUR. Was that money I saw you with?

BARON. Just a few hundred marks which I need for a little trip to—

CHAUFFEUR. Every little bit helps. *(HE digs into the Baron's pocket.)*

BARON. *(Fighting him off.)* No! That's only a pittance to your people, it's everything to me! Everything! No!

CHAUFFEUR. *(Pocketing the Baron's money.)* Here's a tip, Baron. If I was you I'd crawl into room 420—a certain randy businessman will be next door playing with his little blonde secretary. I saw his wallet, stuffed with fifty-mark notes. Stuffed! Here, you better take this. *(HE offers his gun.)*

BARON. I won't need it—

CHAUFFEUR. Take it! This is your last chance.

(The BARON pockets the gun and slowly follows CHAUFFEUR Off.)

COMPANY.
H-A-P-P-Y
WHY, WHY AM I SO HAPPY?
WHEN THEY PLAY THE CHARLESTON,
CHARLESTON, CHARLESTON?

H-A-P-P-Y WHY, WHY AM I SO HAPPY
WHEN THEY PLAY THE CHARLESTON,
CHARLESTON, CHARLESTON, CHARLESTON,
CHARLESTON, CHARLESTON, CHARLESTON,
  [etc.]

(LIGHTS up on Flaemmchen's room where FLAEMMCHEN is still dancing for PREYSING.

*In the Broadway production the COMPANY formed a
line to indicate a wall between the two rooms. The
BARON is seen climbing into Preysing's room.)*

PREYSING. What muscles modern girls have!
Almost like boys. But not quite. (*Laughs.*)
FLAEMMCHEN. Is your daughter younger than
me?
PREYSING. Much younger. Take off your dress.
FLAEMMCHEN. No! It's cold!
PREYSING. (*Dangerously.*) Take off your—
FLAEMMCHEN. What?
PREYSING. (*HE pantomimes wriggling out of
underpants.*) You know—

*(HE watches as SHE reluctantly slips off her panties and
kicks them aside.)*

PREYSING. There, that wasn't so difficult, was it?
Now come sit on my lap and be nice to me. (*HE pulls her
down onto his lap.*) Listen, there are funny little things I
want you to do—(*HE whispers in her ear.*)
FLAEMMCHEN. "Funny little things"! Does your
wife do that?
PREYSING. Do not mention my wife again, not
ever again, hear me?
FLAEMMCHEN. (*Trying to pull away.*) Look, I've
made a bad mistake, I have to go home! Let me go!
Mister Preysing!!

*(Her voice has risen—In next room, the BARON
recognizes her voice—comes slightly Downstage,
listening.)*

PREYSING. We made a business arrangement, now
hold still!
FLAEMMCHEN. Let me go, I can't do this! LET
ME GO!

(The BARON steps into the room.)

BARON. Flaemmchen, get your things and leave.
PREYSING. (*Wheeling, furious.*) What the hell are you doing here?
BARON. It's all right, Flaemmchen. Go home.
PREYSING. What business is this of yours? Get out of my room!
BARON. This isn't *your* room, is it? You're in no position to be giving orders, Mister General Director Preysing.
PREYSING. (*Looks at them both.*) Of course—I understand now. This is some sort of blackmail! I've seen you dancing together!—you're confederates!
FLAEMMCHEN. No, no! He has nothing to do with this!

(MUSIC CUE #16A: PRE-DEATH)

PREYSING. Wait a minute—that's *my* room you came out of—what were you doing in my room?
BARON. Nothing. The night clerk let me into the wrong room.
PREYSING. My *money's* in there! Let's just see what you were doing—(*Moving quickly, PREYSING crosses to the Baron and pushes him into connecting room. Their VOICES are heard from Off.*)
BARON. (*Offstage.*) Take your hands off me!
PREYSING. (*Offstage.*) That's my wallet! All the money for my trip! You're nothing but a dirty, common thief! Give me back my wallet!
FLAEMMCHEN. (*Running Off into Preysing's room.*) No—he isn't a thief! He's a baron!

(The following lines overlap.)

PREYSING. (*Offstage.*) I'm calling the police!

BARON. (*Offstage.*) No! Stand back! Let go! Let go!
FLAEMMCHEN. (*Offstage.*) For God's sake,
Mister Preysing—*don't*—No!
BARON. (*Offstage.*) Good God, man!

(*A shot is heard—silence for a moment—and then
FLAEMMCHEN runs out of Preysing's room and
Downstage. SHE is screaming. MUSIC covers with a
screaming sound.*)

FLAEMMCHEN. Help! Help! We need a doctor!
(*SHE runs Off, frantic.*)
DOCTOR. He was shot right through the heart. A
bull's-eye. What is sometimes called a lucky shot. Not so
lucky for one more fallen young man.

(MUSIC CUE #16B: ROSES AT THE STATION)

(*The LIGHTING changes—the GHOST OF THE
BARON, still wearing evening clothes, appears well
Upstage; HE sings what were his dying thoughts as
RAILWAY STATION PEOPLE form around him, and
freeze ... HE comes slowly Downstage as HE sings.*)

BARON.
I'M HERE, ELIZAVETA, AT THE STATION.
HERE WITH THE ROSES AT THE STATION.
I'M HERE, ELIZAVETA, AT THE STATION.
HERE WITH THE ROSES AT THE STATION.

ALL MY LIFE I HAVE WANTED TO BE HERE,
ALL MY LIFE I HAVE WAITED TO APPEAR
AT THE STATION
WITH THESE ROSES!

I'M HERE, ELIZAVETA, AT THE STATION.
HERE WITH THE ROSES AT THE STATION.

HERE IN MY MIND
WITH THE SECONDS RUNNING OUT ON MY LIFE,
WITH THE SECONDS RUNNING OUT ON MY LIFE
I'M AS CLOSE AS I'LL EVER GET TO YOU
AT THE STATION ...!

PREYSING, WHY DID YOU STRUGGLE FOR THE
GUN?
WHY DID YOU NEED TO HAVE YOUR WALLET?
WHY DID YOU NEED TO KEEP YOUR WALLET?
WHY DID YOU KILL ME FOR YOUR WALLET?
WHY?

(The PASSENGERS begin to disperse.)

BARON.
ELIZAVETA, I AM HERE AT THE STATION,
HERE WITH YOU, DEAR, AT THE STATION,
HERE WITH THE ROSES AT THE STATION.

ALL MY LIFE I HAVE LIVED AS I WANTED TO,
ALL MY LIFE I HAVE HAD EVERYTHING
THAT I WANTED ...!
I SPENT MY CHILDHOOD IN THE FIELDS,
MY BOYHOOD ON HORSEBACK,
I WAS A SOLDIER IN THE WAR:
THE BULLETS WHIZZED PAST MY EAR
BUT NOT ONE CAME NEAR ME
TILL NOW ...
TILL NOW!

*(Blood appears on his shirt-front—enough to run down
and turn some of his shirt red.)*

BARON.
ELIZAVETA,
LOVE CAN'T HAPPEN QUITE SO QUICKLY,
NOT UNLESS I DREAMED YOU

BEAUTIFULLY AND SWEETLY …

I'M HERE, ELIZAVETA, AT THE STATION.
HERE WITH THE ROSES AT THE STATION
RED ROSES—
FOR PASSION—
AT THE STATION!
(Growing faint.)
WHERE ARE YOU? WHERE ARE YOU?

I CAN'T SEE YOU—
I CAN'T SEE YOU …!

(A SHOT is heard. HE backs up, weakly; HE staggers backward to Upstage wall and falls dead. In the Broadway production, this scene ended with an adagio dance, as follows:)

(POSSIBLE CUT)

DOCTOR. And once again, those two sworn enemies, love and death, come face to face and join hands.

(MUSIC CUE #17: DEATH/BOLERO)

(Begin music of a Bolero version of "WHAT YOU NEED." In background PORTERS carry out the BARON's corpse as two dancers—GIGOLO and COUNTESS—dance a sensual, acrobatic adagio miming flirtation, passion, rejection of her by him, abject pleading by her, and finally her death.)

BRIEF BLACKOUT.

SCENE 19

(MUSIC CUE #20: HOW CAN I TELL HER)

Indications of separate rooms in the hotel:
In separate pools of light appear RAFFAELA;
ZINNOWITZ with a POLICE OFFICER or
DETECTIVE; FLAEMMCHEN with KRINGELEIN.

RAFFAELA.
HOW CAN I TELL HER
THIS EARTH-MOVING
   NEWS?
WHAT CAN I SAY?
HOW WILL SHE FEEL?

ZINNOWITZ.
Officer, don't you see? Any word of this could ruin Mister Preysing's life! Just because he defended himself from a hotel thief—

POLICE OFFICER.
Hotel thief?! The deceased was an aristocrat, a Baron!

HOW CAN I TELL HER
WHAT FATE SAYS SHE
   MUST LOSE?
THIS TRUTH, SO
   CRUEL,
MUST I REVEAL?

KRINGELEIN.
He was friendly to me as no man ever.

FLAEMMCHEN.
I can't get him out of my mind.

KRINGELEIN.
And then a piggish man like Mister Preysing kills him.

FLAEMMCHEN.
Yes, Mister Preysing's a complete swine, Otto.

KRINGELEIN.
Why would you agree to go with a man like that?

FLAEMMCHEN.
I wanted to get out.

(DETECTIVE is leading PREYSING out.)

PREYSING.
Please, I want to wash my hands—I must wash them!

(But DETECTIVE pushes him along.)

FLAEMMCHEN.
—He was going to give me a thousand marks. Enough for me to start a new life.

KRINGELEIN.
I never realized how important money was until I saw what it could buy.

FLAEMMCHEN.
Do you mean me?

KRINGELEIN.
You were going with him for money. Yes.

FLAEMMCHEN.
Well, people come to that. When you've been without a job, and your clothes are all out of date, and you can't bear where you live—

KRINGELEIN.
If you could go away with him, hating him—

FLAEMMCHEN.
You're right, Mister Kringelein—I've just got to find some other way! (*SHE goes.*)

KRINGELEIN.
(*Alone, HE finishes the sentence, without realizing she's gone.*) — Flaemmchen, I have money!—Quite a bit of money—thanks to our late friend—(*HE turns and sees that he's alone.*)

RAFFAELA.
IS IT WISER SHE NOT
   KNOW?
HOW CAN I TELL HER
THIS TALE SO HEAVY
   WITH HEARTBREAK:
HER NEW-FOUND
   LOVER
SO SOON IS GONE!

HOW CAN I TELL
   HER?—
I CAN'T!

KRINGELEIN.
He was so young—so handsome—

SCENE 20

(MUSIC CUE #21: FINAL SCENE – PART I)

The Lobby. Early morning. The OPERATORS are at their switchboard as their bells ring.

OPERATORS.
Grand Hotel, at your service—
Grand Hotel, at your service—
Grand Hotel, at your service—
COMPANY. *(Singing.)*
GRAND HOTEL, BERLIN!
ERIK. *(Answers the phone.)* Good morning, Grand Hotel, front desk—This is Erik Litnauer ... would I like to speak to my wife? God, yes! You mean she's right there?—Yes, I'll wait.
COMPANY.
GRAND HOTEL, BERLIN!
ERIK. Gretchen, dearest!—What?—Oh, thank God, I'm so happy, so relieved—should you be talking?—I can't hear you, what's that noise?—You mean that's *him*? That's our son? Gretchen—bring him close to the phone—Hello, son. We haven't even thought up a name for you yet—Son, you're going to have everything— *everything*! I'm going to make sure of that! *(Sings.)*
WELCOME TO LIFE!
WELCOME, WELCOME, YOUNG—ERIK!
YOU WARM THE WORLD,
GIVE THE MORNING A GLOW!

(PREYSING crosses in handcuffs, being led by the DETECTIVE.)

PREYSING. Isn't there a back way out of here? A less public way?

(The DETECTIVE ignores him, takes him out the revolving door, followed by ZINNOWITZ.)

ERIK.
YOU BRING NEW LIGHT
TO A DAY THAT WAS DARK'NING!
WELCOME, MY SON—!
YOU'LL GROW TO BE A STURDY BOY
BECAUSE OF HOW WE WILL LIVE!
I'LL SHOW YOU ALL THE BOUNDLESS JOY,
THE JOY THAT LIVING CAN GIVE,
LOVING CAN GIVE!

(KRINGELEIN, carrying his own luggage, appears and passes the Doctor.)

DOCTOR. Leaving, Kringelein?

KRINGELEIN. Yes—and I want to thank you, Colonel-Doctor. And say goodbye.

DOCTOR. What's wrong, Kringelein—didn't you find "Life" at Grand Hotel?

KRINGELEIN. In a way, yes I did. I'm luckier than our poor friend, the Baron.

DOCTOR. Yes, it's a pity. He seemed to like being alive.

KRINGELEIN. Excuse me, I have to settle my bill—*(HE crosses the lobby, presumably to the cashier.)*

(WITT appears, followed by SANDOR, and approaches ROHNA.)

WITT. She's on her way down. Madame Grushinskaya is on her way down. Listen, if she asks about Baron von Gaigern, not a *word* about what has happened—she must know nothing about that. She has a performance to give in Vienna. *(Hands him money.)*

ROHNA. Yes, sir. You can depend on it.

SANDOR. My God, what's keeping her? She must not miss the express! Bring her car around front—

ROHNA. (*Calling.*) Madame Grushinskaya's car!

DOORMAN. Madame Grushinskaya's car!

ERIK.
LIFE CAN BE GRAND,
WIDE AND HIGH AS THE HEAVENS!
LIFE CAN BE SMALL
AS A SEED IN THE SAND!
IT'S ALL YOURS TO COMMAND!

(FLAEMMCHEN enters.)

KRINGELEIN. Hello, Miss Flaemmchen—you came back.

FLAEMMCHEN. Yes. I forgot my typewriter. I'll need it a little while longer, I'm afraid.

KRINGELEIN. Guess what. I'm going to Paris!

FLAEMMCHEN. Really? I've never seen Paris.

KRINGELEIN. Neither have I.

FLAEMMCHEN. I'm mad about travelling. Not that I could ever afford it.

KRINGELEIN. Well, I'd ask you to come with me—but, you see, I'm a dying man.

FLAEMMCHEN. (*Laughing.*) We're all dying, Otto. *(SHE exits to get her typewriter.)*

KRINGELEIN. (*Mostly to himself.*) Yes. That's true, isn't it?

(GRUSHINSKAYA enters the lobby.)

GRUSHINSKAYA. Oh, Hans, thank you so much. (*Tips Hans.*)

RAFFAELA. Madame, there you are. We must hurry, Madame.

GRUSHINSKAYA. I cannot leave yet. Call his room, Raffaela. Where is he? I left him word what time—

RAFFAELA. Please, we must go, Elizaveta, dearest.

(GRUSHINSKAYA looks at her in surprise.)

RAFFAELA. What? Did I call you "Elizaveta dearest"? I'm sorry. But of course it's only natural. After all these years. *(Deliberately.)* Come, Elizaveta, he will be at the station.
GRUSHINSKAYA. *(Remembering.)* The station! Of course! I remember now. He told me he will be at the railway station with his arms full of roses—he will be there, won't he?
RAFFAELA. Of course he will.
GRUSHINSKAYA. Red roses for passion—
RAFFAELA. *(Putting her arm and cape around her.)* Yes, Elizaveta, dearest, for passion. Come along now.

(THEY go out through the revolving door. KRINGELEIN has joined the DOCTOR who has just whispered something to him.)

KRINGELEIN. —No, no, Doctor, Flaemmchen's not like that, Doctor!
DOCTOR. Don't be a fool, Kringelein—She would leave you the minute your money ran out. Then where would "Life" be?
KRINGELEIN. Where it's never been before—Behind me.

(DOCTOR laughs.
FLAEMMCHEN re-enters, carrying typewriter.)

KRINGELEIN. *(To Doctor.)* There she is. Excuse me. *(Crosses to Flaemmchen and stops her.)* Flaemmchen—would you come to Paris with me? They say it's very pretty.
FLAEMMCHEN. Good Lord, you've got a way with you. Good Lord!
KRINGELEIN. Will you come?

FLAEMMCHEN. You're awfully sweet, Otto—but I must tell you the truth. I'm afraid I'm pregnant.

KRINGELEIN. Afraid? (*Takes her typewriter.*) But that's wonderful! I've never held a newborn baby—that's certainly something to look forward to. So I'll ask you again—*will* you come to Paris?

FLAEMMCHEN. Oh, Otto—I'm at such loose ends!—Don't ask me—tell me!

KRINGELEIN. (*HE looks around, straightens his shoulders, then sings.*)
FRAULEIN FLAEMMCHEN,
YOU WILL COME TO PARIS. [Par-ee]
YOU'LL BE TAKING THE TRAIN THERE
NEXT TO ME!

FLAEMMCHEN. Oh, Otto—How can I refuse!

(*THEY start Up toward revolving door.*)

ERIK. (*To Kringelein.*) Sir—I have a son!

KRINGELEIN. A son?

ERIK. Yes, sir. Just born!

KRINGELEIN. You see? Life is everywhere! Give him this—(*Hands him the Baron's cigarette case.*)—from our friend, the Baron. Please take it. And *mazel tov*!

ERIK. (*Looks around first.*) *Mazel tov* to you too, sir. (*Turns.*) Taxi for his Excellency, Mister Kringelein!

DOORMAN. Taxi for his Excellency, Mister Kringelein!

FLAEMMCHEN. (*Delighted.*) Taxi for his Excellency, Mister Kringelein!

(*KRINGELEIN and FLAEMMCHEN exit through revolving door Up; Lights begin to dim; DOCTOR walks purposefully to Downstage Center and says to audience.*)

DOCTOR. I'll stay—one more day.

(After a moment, perhaps with\a burst of STEAM, perhaps with a CRASH of crockery, the SCULLERY WORKERS enter and sing.)

(MUSIC CUE #21A: FINAL SCENE—PART II)

SCULLERY #1. God!
SCULLERY #2. Work!
SCULLERY WORKERS.
SOME HAVE, SOME HAVE NOT!
SOME HAVE, SOME HAVE NOT!
SOME HAVE, SOME HAVE NOT!
WHY?

EVERY BUM AND BITCH IN ALL BERLIN IS RICH
  EXCEPT FOR US!
EVERY BUM AND BITCH IN ALL BERLIN IS RICH
  EXCEPT FOR US!
EVERY BUM AND BITCH IN ALL BERLIN IS RICH
  EXCEPT FOR US!

ALL 4 SCULLS.	**ENSEMBLE.**
SOME HAVE, SOME HAVE NOT!	EVERY BUM (ETC.)
3 SCULLS.	
SOME HAVE, SOME HAVE NOT!	EVERY BUM (ETC.)
GUNTHER GUSTAFFSON.	
SOME HAVE, SOME HAVE NOT!	EVERY BUM (ETC.)
SCULLERY WORKERS.	
EVERY BUM—EVERY BITCH—IN ALL BERLIN—	EVERY BUM (ETC.)
IS RICH—EXCEPT— FOR US!	EVERY BUM (ETC.)

SCULLS & ENSEMBLE.
EVERY BUM AND BITCH IN ALL BERLIN IS RICH
 EXCEPT FOR US!
EVERY BUM AND BITCH IN ALL BERLIN IS RICH
 EXCEPT FOR US!
EVERY BUM AND BITCH IN ALL BERLIN IS RICH
 EXCEPT FOR US!
EVERY BUM AND BITCH IN ALL BERLIN IS RICH
 EXCEPT FOR US!
 WHY?

(MUSIC CUE #21B: GRAND ENDING)

DOCTOR. Grand Hotel, Berlin. Always the same—people come, people go—One life ends while another begins—one heart breaks while another beats faster—one man goes to jail while another goes to Paris—always the same.

(The COMPANY sings "The Grand Parade.")

GROUP #1.	**GROUP #2.**
GRAND HOTEL,	AT THE GRAND,
GRAND HOTEL,	YOU ARE AT THE GRAND!
MUSIC CONSTANTLY PLAYING!	AT THE GRAND,
GRAND HOTEL,	YOU ARE AT THE GRAND!
LIVING WELL!	AT THE GRAND, YOU ARE AT THE GRAND HOTEL!

AH-----------------
ROUND AND ROUND
AH-----------------
 DOCTOR. The revolving door turns and turns—and life goes on.

GROUP #1.	GROUP #2.
IT'S THE DIN	AT THE GRAND,
OF OLD BERLIN!	YOU ARE AT THE
	GRAND!
YOU'RE IN THE	AT THE GRAND,
GRAND HOTEL!	
GRAND HOTEL,	YOU ARE AT THE
	GRAND!
GRAND HOTEL,	AT THE GRAND,
GRAND HOTEL (ETC.)	YOU ARE AT THE
	GRAND HOTEL (ETC.)

CURTAIN

CURTAIN CALLS

(MUSIC CUE #22: GRAND WALTZ)

COMPANY.
AND LIFE GOES ON,
ROUND 'N' ROUND,
BACK 'N' FORTH,
ON AND ON!
WE AND YOU
PARADING THROUGH
THE GRAND CAFE,
NONCHALANTLY
TABLE-HOPPING
LIFE AWAY!
DAY TO NIGHT,
DARK TO DAWN,
COME 'N' GONE,
BACK 'N' FORTH,
EAST 'N' WEST,
SOUTH 'N' NORTH,
LIFE GOES ON!

THE END

COSTUME NOTES

BARON FELIX VON GAIGERN

2 pc. Suit
Vest
Shirt
Cape
Gloves
Shoes

2 pc. Suit
Shirt
Shoes

Russian Peasant Shirt
(for climb into Grushinskaya's suite)

2 pc. Tuxedo
Brocade Vest
Wing-Tip Shirt
Patent Shoes

THE DOCTOR

3 pc. Suit
Shirt
Boots w/Leg Brace

KRINGELEIN

Distressed 3 pc. Suit
Shirt
Boots
Old Overcoat
Old Hat
Old Sweater Vest

2 pc. Tuxedo
Brocade Vest
Shoes
Wing-tip Shirt

New 3 pc. Suit
New Shirt
New Fur-Collared Overcoat
New Boots
New Hat

PREYSING

2 pc. Suit
Shirt
Shoes
Fur-Collared Overcoat

2 pc. Tuxedo
Wing-Tip Shirt
Shoes

ZINNOWITZ

3 pc. Suit
Shirt
Shoes
Overcoat

SANDOR

3 pc. Suit
Shirt
Shoes
Spats
Fur-Collared Overcoat
Hat

WITT

3 pc. Suit
Shirt
Shoes
Spats
Caped Overcoat
Hat

CHAUFFEUR

Uniform Jacket
Uniform Jodhpurs
Boots
Uniform Cap

ROHNA

Uniform Tail Coat
Uniform Vest
Uniform pants
Shirt
Shoes
Spats

ERIK

Uniform Tailcoat
Uniform Vest
Uniform Pants
Shirt
Shoes
Spats

THE GIGOLO

2 pc. Suit	Russian Peasant Shirt
Vest	(for Bolero)
Shirt	Dance Trousers
Shoes	Shoes

THE DOORMAN

Uniform Topcoat
Trousers
Uniform Hat
Boots
Gloves
Shirt

BELLBOYS

Uniform Jackets	Overcoat	(contd.)

Uniform Vests   Civilian Hat
Uniform Pants
Uniform Hat
Boots
Gloves
Shirts

THE TWO JIMMYS

Uniform Jacket   Suit Jacket
Vest   Vest
Trousers   Trousers
Sash   Shirt
Shirt   Overcoat
Hat   Cap
Shoes   Shoes

SCULLERY WORKERS AS STOCKHOLDERS

Suit Jacket
Suit Trousers
Shirt
Hat
Shoes

DETECTIVE

Trench Coat

SCULLERY WORKER #2

Distressed Apron
Ragged Pants
Leather Coat
Boots
Cap
Gloves

SCULLERY WORKER #3

Pants
Leather Coat
Boots
Gloves

SCULLERY WORKER #4

Pants
Assorted Head, Wrist, and Neck Rags
Distressed Tee Shirt
Boots

GRUSHINSKAYA

Full-length Dress w/Fur Trim
Fur Stole
Hat
Shoes

Rehearsal Tutu and
Bodice
Pointe Shoes
Shawl

Performance Tutu and Bodice
Ballet Slippers
Lace Shawl

Full-length Dress
Fur Wrap
Hat w/Fur Trim

RAFFAELA

Blouse
Skirt/Pants
Vest
Coat
Cape
Fedora
Boots

Oriental Pajama Pants
Oriental Pajama Top
Slipper Flats

FLAEMMCHEN

Dress w/Slip
Coat
Hat
Handbag
Shoes

Dress w/Slip
Stockings
Garter Belt
Tap Pants

MADAME PEEPEE

Dress
Oversmock
Coat
Boots
Hat

2 pc. Dress
Apron
Cardigan

TELEPHONE OPERATORS

Dress
Shoes
Maid's Hat
Maid's Apron
Overcoat

Stockholder's Overcoat
Hat

HOTEL COURTESAN

Dress
Repeat Operator Shoes
Jacket

COUNTESS

Evening Gown
Hat
Shoes

Full-length Dress
(for Bolero)
No Shoes (for Bolero)

PROPS PRESET ON STAGE

4 SCULLERY BASKETS OF CROCKERY: In House
Right aisle for SCULLERY WORKERS to enter from
auditorium

REVOLVING DOOR: DSC—Check gear release US and
set in down position

CHAIRS: 40 chairs on stage
                       2 weighted stairs on SR side
                       3 chairs – 1 quick change chair
                               USR
                       4 extra chairs off SL

LADDER: DR in offstage position

NEWSPAPER: USR pillar

DOCTOR BAG WITH SYRINGE & TOURNIQUET:
DSR stool

PERIOD MOVIE MAG FOR FLAEMMCHEN: DSR
Proscenium

CARPETS: Offstage and curled under

BRAILE BOOK: USR in box

SUITCASES   10 GRUSHINSKAYA. cases SR
                     1 FLAEMM SIT SR prop table
                     2 KRINGELEIN cases SL

THE BAR: USC in trough

DIME NOVEL: USR trough

TELEPHONE & SHELF: Off USL

THE DUSTMOP: Preset USL

ASHTRAYS w/WATER: All four pillars

BARON'S CIGARETTE: DSR pillar

GUN: On pillar USR

STAGE RIGHT PROP TABLE

Period Typewriter with paper
Stretcher
FLAEMM's sit suitcase
Handcuffs for Preysing
Bar Towel – Double
Extra syringe & tourniquet
ZINNOWITZ's briefcase

STAGE LEFT PROP TABLE

RAFFAELA's purse with jewels
PREYSING's briefcase
Cigarettes & Lighters & Matches
DOCTOR's tourniquet
8 Bathroom towels
Radiogram
4 Bar towels
SANDOR's briefcase
Dust pan & Small broom
1 Apron (wardrobe – Erik.)
Cane – for DOCTOR
Music
Papers for meeting
Money – Real & Fake
KRINGELEIN's 2 battered suitcases

PERSONAL PROPS

KRINGELEIN
Pen
Wallet with marks
2 suitcases hard money

PREYSING
Briefcase with papers, etc.
Wallet with marks and picture
Small (2-1/2" X 4") leather notebook
Pen
Cigar case with cigars
Lighter

FLAEMMCHEN
Typewriter and paper
Movie magazines
1 suitcase

ZINNOWITZ
Briefcase with meeting minutes (for Flaemmchen) and
Papers
Money clip
Soft marks
Cigarette case
Lighter
Pocket comb

WITT
Account book
Pen
Cigarette case
Lighter

SANDOR
Folder-type valise with misc. papers
Wallet

Marks
Posters
Theatre tickets
Train timetable
Newspaper

MADAME PEEPEE
Bathroom towels
Cigarettes

ROHNA
Pack of cigarettes
Lighter
Pwatch
Key chain (Grand)

CHAUFFEUR
Gun with blanks

BARON
Gold cigarette case with jewelled clasp
Lighter

RAFFAELA
Grushinskaya's necklace
Valise
Grushinskaya's ballet slippers

GIGOLO
Cigarette case
Lighter

MISC.
Radiograms (SR)
Pushbroom (duster)(SL)
Small broom and dustpan (SL)
Bar towels
Cigarette packs

Matches
Lighters

Preset for SR operator to set on stage:

Marks SR for Baron's room
Tie pin
Clothes

LUTHER DAVIS

GRAND HOTEL – THE MUSICAL exists because Luther Davis wandered into a second-hand bookstore some years ago and picked up a copy of Vicki Baum's (by then out of print) novel. He was still enjoying his share of the fruits of his successful collaboration with Charles Lederer and Wright and Forrest on the musical KISMET and thought that GRAND HOTEL would be a worthy successor. He negotiated for the rights, wrote a musical book, and enlisted Wright and Forrest to create the score. Together Wright, Forrest and Davis have organized two productions based on Vicki Baum's novel—an early and quite different one called AT THE GRAND for the Los Angeles and San Francisco Light Opera Associations, and the present one. In addition to KISMET and GRAND HOTEL – The Musical, he has written for the stage the play KISS THEM FOR ME (Broadway), the musical TIMBUKTU! (Broadway—he also produced it.) and the plays THEY VOTED YES and CHANGING THE WORLD (Regional theaters). He has written fifteen movies, many television specials, and co-produced off Broadway Stephen MacDonald's play NOT ABOUT HEROES. He has been nominated for three Tonys and won one, won two Mystery Writers of America Edgar Allan Poe awards, and many Writers Guild nominations. He says he is "an earnest member" of the Dramatists Guild, the Writers Guild of America, and the League of American Theaters and Producers. He is the father of two and an enthusiastic supporter of Zero Population Growth.

ROBERT WRIGHT AND GEORGE FORREST

Since meeting at age 15 in Miami Senior High School (their first song, "Hail to Miami High!"), Wright and Forrest have enjoyed one of the most enduring and productive partnerships in music, theater and motion pictures. Since signing a seven-year composer-lyricist contract with Metro-Goldwyn-Mayer at ages 20 and 21, they have received collaborative credit for lyrics, music, and/or musical adaptation for 60 films, 18 produced stage musicals, numerous stage and cabaret revues, 13 television spectaculars, numerous radio programs, etc.

Films, mostly for M-G-M, many starring Jeanette MacDonald and Nelson Eddy: MAYTIME; SWEETHEARTS; THE FIREFLY; BALALAIKA, I MARRIED AN ANGEL; BROADWAY SERENADE; LET FREEDOM SING; MANNEQUIN; MUSIC IN MY HEART; DANCE, GIRL, DANCE; SARATOGA; KISMET; SONG OF NORWAY; THE GREAT WALTZ, etc.

Stage: SONG OF NORWAY; MAGDALENA; THE GREAT WALTZ; KISMET; KEAN; ANYA; TIMBUKTU!; GRAND HOTEL, The Musical, etc.

Songs: "The Donkey Serenade"; "At the Balalaika"; "Always and Always"; "It's A Blue World"; "Stranger in Paradise"; "Strange Music"; "Baubles, Bangles and Beads"; "And This is My Beloved"; "'Night of My Nights"; "The Olive Tree"; "Sweet Danger"; "Willow, Willow, Willow"; "The Fog and the Grog"; "Bubble, Bubble, Bubble"; "Sands of Time", etc.

Stage Revues: THANK YOU, COLUMBUS; FUN FOR YOUR MONEY; ZIEGFELD FOLLIES (1942); ARTISTS AND MODELS; FOLIES BERGERE; RED,

WHITE AND BLUE; eleven Camp Tamiment Revues, etc.

Television: 13 STAR TIME spectaculars starring Benny Goodman, Frances Langford, Lou Parker, Dick Haymes, etc.

Cabaret: 6 Copacabana revues starring Jimmy Durante, Perry Como, Ella Logan, Frank Fay, Jane Froman, Sophie Tucker, etc; 3 Colonial Inn Casino revues starring Ray Bolger, Carmen Miranda, Joe E. Lewis, Jane Froman, Gwen Verdon, Jack Cole, The Kraft Sisters, Jack Cole Dancers.

Radio: Vick's Radio Hour starring Nelson Eddy; M-G-M's Maxwell House GOOD NEWS, starring Fanny Brice, Judy Garland, Allan Jones, Sophie Tucker, Meredith Willson, etc; U.S. TREASURY STAR PARADE starring Fredric March, Janet Gaynor, Al Goodman, John Green, etc.

Awards: 3 Motion Picture Oscar Nominations, Best Song: "It's A Blue World" (MUSIC IN MY HEART); "Always and Always" (MANNEQUIN); "Pennies for Peppino" (FIESTA). Antoinette Perry (TONY) Award: Best Score — KISMET; 4 Drama Desk and TONY nominations, Music and Lyrics — GRAND HOTEL.

Artists in Residence: Boston University, University of Alabama, University of Michigan, Hope College. Adjunct Professors: University of Miami, Florida.

Current Projects: BETTING ON BERTIE, Book and Lyrics by P.G. Wodehouse and Guy Bolton; A SONG FOR CYRANO; THE ANASTASIA AFFAIRE, LA VIE and a musical version of Eudora Welty's "The Ponder Heart," all three with Books by Jerome Chodorov. FRIENDS ... AND STRANGERS IN PARADISE, a

Concert Revue featuring a retrospective of Wright and Forrest compositions from 1935 to 1993.

Wright and Forrest reside on Biscayne Bay, in Miami, Florida and near Carnegie Hall in Manhattan.